Convinced of God's
LOVE

Growing in Humility and Worship

Tony R. Guinn

Convinced of God's Love: Growing in Humility and Worship
Copyright© 2010 by Tony R. Guinn
Revised 2015
Previously subtitled *Growing in Humility and Security*

All Scripture quotations, unless otherwise indicated, are taken from the *Holy Bible: New International Version®*. NIV®. Copyright© 1973, 1978, 1984 by International Bible Society. Used by permission of Zondervan. All rights reserved.

All rights reserved. No part of this publication may be reproduced, stored in a retrieval system, or transmitted in any form or by any means—electronic, mechanical, photocopy, recording, or any other—except for brief quotations in printed reviews, without the prior permission of the author. All inquiries should be addressed to Tony R. Guinn via e-mail at jcdied4hisown@gmail.com.

Printed in the United States of America

Book Cover Design and Art Direction: Dorinda Guinn
Proofreading: Dorinda Guinn, Mary Harris, and Brian Retz.
Interior Design and Layout: Dorinda Guinn

Table of Contents

    Acknowledgments   5
    Preface   7

1. You Need to Be Convinced!   9
2. Pride/Idolatry   17
3. In Christ   31
4. What You Do or Your Standing?   45
5. Live for God's Glory!   61
6. God Is for You!   73
7. Being Convinced in Trials   83
8. For I Am Convinced!   95
9. Love According to God   113
10. God's Love Changes Everything   121
11. May You Be Convinced!   141

    References   153

Acknowledgments

To Dorinda, my wife, thank you for your encouragement and countless hours spent reading, editing, proofreading, and designing this book. You are a true helper suitable for me as God intended.

I also give my sincere thanks to all of those who have spoken encouraging words and have helped me in a variety of ways during the writing of this book.

Preface

Has the statement "God loves you" lost its sense of wonder? Or do you meditate on the transforming truth that in Christ you are perfectly loved by God? Until we are convinced that "nothing can separate us from the love of God in Christ Jesus," our relationship with God and with others will never be what it can be.

We all struggle with sinful pride. In our pride we reject what God says in his word. When we reject what God says in his word, we sin and we worship any number of different idols. In our idolatry, we worship the creation rather than the Creator. However, when we are consumed with and controlled by the perfect love of God, we are humbled. When we are humble, we live for God's glory and worship him, rather than living for our own glory and worshipping people (including ourselves), places, and things.

In this book you will gain a deeper understanding of God's love. You will see why you can be convinced of his love, and how being convinced of his love will transform your life.

At the end of each chapter there are questions to consider and suggested prayers. For individual study you can use these questions as a time for personal reflection and prayer. For a small group study you can use these questions for group discussion and prayer. As you become more convinced of

God's love, seek to encourage others by sharing with them how God's love is transforming your life. I hope and pray that you will find this an enjoyable, enlightening, encouraging, helpful, and Christ-glorifying book.

Chapter 1

You Need to Be Convinced!

On a daily basis there are countless messages coming at us from many different sources which tell us that we need to be convinced of what they are saying. The marketing strategies of various companies attempt to draw our attention to the benefits of their products to meet our physical needs (such as food, water, clothing, and shelter), "felt needs," or "needs" that we did not even know existed. In addition to product advertising, various philosophies and many different subcultures compete for our attention. As if all of this were not enough, those in our sphere of relationships also try to convince us of what they think we need.

Do I want you to be convinced of something? Yes. Why? Because rightly understood and applied it will radically change your life for the glory of God. God has given those of us in Christ an amazing, incredible, overwhelming, unchanging, and humbling promise.

What is this amazing promise that we need to be convinced of that will help us to grow to be more like Christ? God has promised that if we are in Christ nothing can separate us from his love. If you are in Christ, which means you are spiritually united to Christ through faith, you need to be convinced of God's amazing promise concerning his love for you.[1] By what authority can I say that you need to be convinced of this promise? The answer to that question is simple. God made sure this promise was written in his word. So obviously, according to God, you need to know this promise and trust in it. Having this promise firmly fixed in your mind and heart will help you to become increasingly conformed to the likeness of Christ.

My prayer is that after reading this book, you will be able to say with genuine confidence that you firmly believe that nothing can separate you from the love of God in Christ Jesus. More important than what I desire for you is what God desires for you. He wants you to be as assured as the Apostle Paul was in the eighth chapter of Romans when he wrote under the inspiration of the Holy Spirit, "For I am *convinced* that neither death nor life, neither angels nor demons, neither the present nor the future, nor any powers, neither height nor depth, nor anything else in all creation, will be able to separate us from the love of God that is *in Christ* Jesus our Lord" (Romans 8:38-39, emphasis mine).

What does Paul mean when he writes of being convinced? He means to believe, to trust, or to have faith. The Bible clearly defines faith for us. "Now faith is being sure of what we hope for and certain of what we do not see" (Hebrews 11:1). As with faith, being convinced means that you are sure and certain that what God says is true. The Reformation Study Bible says it in this way, "Confidence based on the promises of God is the essence of biblical faith."[2]

---

[1] The meaning of being "in Christ" or being united to Christ is discussed in greater detail in Chapter 3, which is titled "In Christ."
[2] R. C. Sproul, ed., *The Reformation Study Bible: English Standard Version* (Lake Mary, FL: Ligonier Ministries, 2005), 298.

Does this book serve a biblical purpose? Scripture tells us:

> I pray that out of his glorious riches he may strengthen you with power through his Spirit in your inner being, so that Christ may dwell in your hearts through faith. And I pray that you, being rooted and established in love, may have power, together with all the saints, to grasp how wide and long and high and deep is the love of Christ, and to know this love that surpasses knowledge—*that* you may be filled to the measure of all the fullness of God. Now to him who is able to do immeasurably more than all we ask or imagine, according to his power that is at work within us, to him be glory in the church and in Christ Jesus throughout all generations for ever and ever! Amen (Ephesians 3:16-21, emphasis mine).

We see from this passage in Ephesians that in order to be filled with the fullness of God, which is the only time it is possible for you to walk in obedience and thus be conformed to the image of Christ, you must know his amazing love that surpasses knowledge. You must be rooted and established in the love of Christ. You must be convinced of his love! The emphasized word, "that," in verse 19 of the Ephesians passage clearly teaches that for us to be filled with the fullness of God it is required that we know what is written before the word "that." And what is written before the word "that" is the importance of being "rooted" and "established" in God's love. So the answer to the question, "Does this book serve a biblical purpose?" is a resounding "Yes!" Please read these verses in Ephesians again slowly. Think about each verse, and praise God for his love.

You will never reach a point of perfection this side of heaven where you trust perfectly in God and his promises at all times. No mere human has ever been completely focused on God, moment-by-moment, every second of every day. Only Jesus Christ, who is fully God and fully man, has lived a perfectly sinless life in thought, word, and deed. He was constantly convinced of the Father's love. You can, however, grow in your assurance that God's promises concerning his love are true. You can have his promises ready for immediate use when the lies from the flesh, the world, and the devil, which seek to destroy you, creep into your mind. The truth can, and will, set you free if you firmly believe that God loves you and you live by faith in the promise of his love.

To better illustrate how we can be convinced of God's love and live by faith in it, imagine that a steady rain is coming down and you do not want to get soaked as you go outside. What is your likely plan of action? You probably grab an umbrella, open it up, and hold it over you so that you do not get wringing wet. By using the umbrella, you show that you trust that it will help keep you dry. You do not just think about how the umbrella will help you stay dry; you show that you trust it by grabbing it and using it. Then, after you hold it over you, you rest under it. You do not hold it over you one moment and then move the umbrella away from you the next (unless, of course, you want to get wet). You know that you are protected from the rain only when you are under the umbrella. Through this whole process of grabbing, opening, and continuing to walk under the umbrella, you are living by faith in it that it will keep you dry.

Umbrellas are a wonderful invention, and often they do help to keep us dry. Umbrellas can, however, tear, fail to work properly, or simply wear out. Yet in spite of these potential difficulties, many people still have enough faith in them to use them. God's promises, on the other hand, are always reliable. They never wear out. They can never fail.

We cannot just say that we believe in God's promises and yet not put them to use, for that would be as useless as leaving the umbrella behind us as we go out into the rain. We are to hide God's promises in our hearts so that when the lies from the flesh, the world, and the devil come raining down upon us, we can remain committed to living out God's truth.

Trusting in God and his promises leads to humility and worship. Trusting in ourselves leads to pride and idolatry and thus chasing after lies and idols. Walking or living by faith in God's promises involves submitting to them, and continuing to trust in them through the power of the Holy Spirit. We are to rest in and under these promises continually as we walk through the downpour of lies that daily rain down on us. We need to be convinced of God's love, rest in his love, and walk in his love.

When you become convinced of God's love for you in Christ, you will trust in it, rest in it, and live it out. I hope this becomes an ever-increasing reality in your life.

Let me make it clear that this book does not contain any power in itself. God's word is the source of truth. The power to transform our lives comes from the Holy Spirit working by and with the word of God in our hearts. May the Holy Spirit take the Scriptures used in this book to plant the seeds of God's promises deep within your heart. For when that happens, you will be motivated to become increasingly conformed to the likeness of Christ.

At this point, you may be thinking that you are already convinced that nothing can separate you from God's love. Maybe for the most part you are convinced. Yet none of us has arrived. Maybe you are not quite as convinced as you think you are. Maybe your understanding of God's love is not biblically balanced and is somewhat superficial. Maybe you are not sure how to apply his love in specific ways to your daily life as it relates to temptation and difficult circumstances. It is one thing for us to say we believe in God and his love. Yet, it is quite another thing to have his love radically change our lives and our relationships. There has to be at least one place in your life where you do not consistently trust in God and his love. I wish I had only one place in my life. I am yet to meet anyone who is totally trusting God in every area of his life all the time. I do not know the specific areas in your life that you struggle with, but I believe that you will become more convinced of God's love as you continue through this book. I suggest sincerely praying that God will make these areas of struggle clear to you because we can so easily deceive ourselves. I am sure that he will answer that prayer. "Humble yourselves before the Lord, and he will lift you up" (James 4:10).

As you read this book please keep at the forefront of your mind and heart that the chief end of man is to glorify God and enjoy him forever.[3] What does being convinced of God's love have to do with glorifying God? Being convinced that God loves you perfectly in Christ will motivate you to live as God commands you to, and when you live as God commands you to, you will you glorify him. God's love can be clearly seen as a motivator to living for his glory in Psalm 115:1, "Not to us, O Lord, not to us but to your name be the glory, because of your love and faithfulness." Being convinced of God's love leads to living for the only reason that you were created, which is to glorify God.

---

[3] The Orthodox Presbyterian Church, *The Westminster Confession of Faith and Catechisms as adopted by The Presbyterian Church in America With Proofs Texts* (Lawrenceville, GA: Christian Education and Publications, 2007), 71.

In addition to fulfilling your primary purpose in life, which is to glorify God, there is also a delightful bonus or by-product to glorifying God. That by-product is that as you glorify God and enjoy him, you will end up enjoying life to the full. Jesus said, "I have come that they may have life, and have it to the full" (John 10:10b). Actually, the only time you will ever experience life to the full is when you are living to glorify God.

Now that you know why being convinced of God's love is so important, may God grant you the grace to become so! In chapter two you will see what keeps us from being convinced, and thus keeps us from growing in Christ.

Questions and Prayer

1. In what areas of your life do you struggle? In what circumstances do you find yourself not being convinced of, not resting in, and not living out God's love?

2. Begin to pray daily that you will become more convinced of God's love, that you will rest in it, and that you will live it out.

Chapter 2

Pride/Idolatry

If you have spent any time at all pulling weeds, you know that if you do not get to the root, you have not solved the problem. The weeds on top of the ground are the superficial problem, but the source of the problem is the roots underground. The roots must be properly taken care of, or the weeds will continue to grow and you will continue to "have victory" only on the surface level. Things may look good on the outside for a while, but you know what lies beneath and is bound to spring up again.

As with weeds in a garden, we must get to the root of our problem, which is sinful pride that often resides in our hearts. Sinful pride can be defined as the setting up of ourselves as our own authority. Any time we think, speak, or act in ways according to our will, instead of submitting to God's will, his authority, and his word, you can be certain there is pride in our heart. Pride is at the root of all sin. When there is pride in our heart, we do not live by faith. When we are not living by faith, we are not worshipping God. When we are not worshipping God, we are worshipping any number of different idols and thus we are sinning.

Pride always leads to idolatry, or the worship of people (including ourselves), places, or things. When (in our pride) we reject God and his word, we always turn to worshipping the creation and thus commit idolatry and spiritual adultery towards God. When we do this, we set aside worshipping the perfectly holy and perfectly loving glorious God, the greatest of all treasures, for worthless idols, which are nothing but fool's gold. In our pride, we exchange God, the spring of living water, for filthy muddy water and broken cisterns that cannot hold water. We exchange Jesus, the bread of life, for molded, stale bread. We exchange the glorious buffet of feasting on God for scraps at the garbage dump. Pride infects our thoughts, words, and actions. Pride feeds idolatry and idolatry feeds pride. Maybe you have never thought of it this way, but idolatry is intimately connected to pride. This connection is evident in the fact that when we sin, in our pride we reject God's Word, and in our idolatry we worship the creation.

For example, God commands us to serve others. Yet in our pride we often reject God's command to serve others. When we do this we worship the idol of self and we serve ourselves instead of serving others. When we do this, God is not glorified, and in our foolishness we even end up stealing a blessing from ourselves. The Bible says, "It is more blessed to give than to receive" (Acts 20:35). Imagine that you are in the midst of getting your daily "to do" list done. Then you look out the window and see that your neighbor needs help. What will you do? Do you continue focusing on yourself and in your pride try to play God by making sure that you get your things done, and thus fail to serve your neighbor? Or do you in humility trust in God's perfect love and worship him knowing that he will see to it that you get done what is really necessary, and thus serve your neighbor in love?

A focus on self, either in arrogance or insecurity (and these two are often, if not always interrelated), finds its root problem in sinful pride. As Dr. Timothy Keller, senior pastor of Redeemer Presbyterian Church in Manhattan, New York writes, "Pride in the form of self-consciousness (the 'inferiority complex') or in the form of self-confidence (the 'superiority complex') will make the incarnational lifestyle impossible."[4] By "incarnational lifestyle," Keller is writing of imitating Christ. Whether we love to think too highly or too lowly of ourselves, the focus is on self, not on God, and not on others. When our focus is on ourselves, rooted in pride, it is impossible to be humble, worship God, and walk in obedience. However, using the example given above concerning God's command to serve others, when we are convinced of God's love for us, we will, in humility, serve others. Is anything more opposed to the character of Jesus than pride? Is anything more consistent with Jesus' character than humility?

Becoming increasingly convinced of God's love, and thus increasingly conformed to the likeness of Christ, requires greater levels of freedom from pride. Pride is our most destructive enemy. We must learn to put off pride and idolatry and put on humility and worship. For this to happen we must have our minds renewed through the truth of Scripture concerning who God is and what he has done for us.

Pride and his ugly brother, idolatry, go hand in hand. In our idolatry we desperately try to "find something" in people, places, and things. In our pride we choose to not be convinced of what God has said. When we choose not to trust God, idolatry, of some sort, is right there hand in hand with pride. Pride and idolatry are, if you will, just a flip of the coin. For this reason I will often refer to the two together as

---

[4] Timothy J. Keller, *Ministries of Mercy: The Call of the Jericho Road*, 2nd Edition (Phillipsburg, NJ: P & R Publishing, 1997), 64.

"pride/idolatry." The root problem of pride/idolatry leads to destructive thoughts, words, and actions. Becoming convinced of God's promises to those in Christ will help free us from these thoughts, words, and actions.

Pride simply does not believe what God has said. Ever since the serpent said to Eve, "You will be like God" (Genesis 3:5) we have made a mess of things. If Adam and Eve had not, in their pride and idolatry, chosen to chase after the lie and disobey God (who is the only one worthy of worship), they would have continued to walk in humility and worship. Ever since the fall in the garden, mankind has been on a desperate and futile search for "fill in the blank..." in the worship of numerous different idols. And by the way, that search is still going on without success. Jesus is the true treasure. He alone is worth giving up everything (Matthew 13:44-46). Only in knowing and worshipping him does one experience "life to the full." Any time we try to "find something" apart from Christ, we step outside of God's will and fall into the sin of idolatry.

Whenever we chase after something that is outside of God's will we are practicing idolatry. It is serving false gods. It is following the example of Adam and Eve standing at the tree of the knowledge of good and evil, and in our pride, making a foolish choice by exchanging God for a worthless idol (Genesis 2:16-17; 3:6-7).

When we sin we are not resting in the perfect love of God in Christ. If we are resting in God's love, we will be humble and we will not exchange the worship of the one true God for the idolatrous worship of people, places, and things.

Romans 1:25 tells us, "They exchanged the truth of God for a lie, and worshipped and served created things rather than the Creator—who is forever praised. Amen."

Ever since the two-sided coin of pride/idolatry entered the human race, man has time and time again exchanged the truth of God for a lie. The truth is that God alone is worthy of worship. The truth is that in worshipping God you will, as a by-product of worshipping him, find all you have been looking for elsewhere. The truth is that God alone loves perfectly at all times. The lie of idolatry is that people, places, and things will satisfy. How foolish we are in our thinking when we buy into these lies!

Consider the macho man who thinks, talks, and acts like the tough guy. Why does he do this? He does this because there is pride in his heart. He is worshipping at the idol of self, the idol of the fear of man, and other possible idols. He has bought into a lie and worshipped the creation rather than the Creator. Being convinced of God's perfect love in Christ will drive this pride out of his heart and lead to humility and the worship of God rather than the worship of himself and others.

On the other hand, consider the woman who thinks, talks, acts, and dresses provocatively and carries herself in the same way. Why does she do this? She does this because there is pride in her heart. She, too, is worshipping at the idol of self, the idol of the fear of man, and other possible idols. She also has bought into a lie and worshipped the creation rather than the Creator. (By the way, she will never find true love in her idolatry. This behavior will not motivate others to love her for who she is as a person or for her character. In the end she will receive nothing but empty lust and heartache). Being convinced of God's perfect love in Christ will drive this pride out of her heart and lead to humility and worship of God rather than the worship of herself and others.

Humble people do not try to impress other people. Proud people do. Those who are resting in God's perfect love do not try to impress anyone by outward appearances, actions, or anything else. Humble people are concerned with pleasing God (2 Corinthians 5:9).

Maybe the two examples above didn't hit home with you, but I guarantee that in some way you have exchanged the truth of God for a lie and worshipped and served the creation rather than the Creator. We all have. We all have tried to impress people in some way. We all have tried to get people to love and accept us in ways that involve the two-sided coin of pride/idolatry. We all struggle with the fear of man on some level. We all have gone outside of God's will in our thoughts, speech, or actions to serve false gods. Consider the following list: Have you served or do you serve false gods through sexual immorality, gangs, drunkenness, drugs, materialism, telling or laughing at dirty jokes, cursing, gossiping, slandering, looking down upon others, being cold toward others, stealing, lying, dishonoring your father and mother, coveting, being angry, murdering, fearing, worrying, taking things into your own hands, not standing up for the truth, not sharing the gospel, or perhaps doing something that looks good outwardly but with improper motives? These are just some of the ways people serve false gods. Has any of these hit home with you? We all have committed idolatry. We all have committed spiritual adultery toward God.

Please do not misunderstand me. It would be a great thing for us to consistently love everyone and for others to love us all the time. God commands us to love others. Loving people is a good thing and receiving love from others is a good thing. However, we are often guilty of turning what is a good thing into an idol. We often sin in order to try to get love from people and we often sin when we do not get love from people. When we rest in the perfect love of God in Christ we will not fall into the sin of the fear of man and thus we will not sin in trying to get love from people and we will not sin when we do not get love from people. This is just one example of making what is a good thing (the love of others) into an idol. God has blessed us with many things that are within his will for us to enjoy, but we must not, in our pride, reject the worship of God and turn to the worship of good things and make them an idol. I think the One who created us knows what is best for his glory and our good. Don't you?

Pride says, "I will get what I want (or what I think I "need") through some person, place, or thing." When this happens, the inward and outward battle of pride/idolatry rears its ugly head. While this is happening, the devil sits back and laughs because he knows the pain and destruction that are coming. "The thief comes only to steal and kill and destroy" (John 10:10a). The devil comes to destroy our lives. Yet, look at what the rest of John 10:10 says, "I have come that they may have life, and have it to the full" (John 10:10b). Jesus has come that we will not only have eternal life but that we can enjoy life to the full. The options are pretty plain. We can listen to Satan's lies and in our pride destroy our lives, or we can listen to God's truth and in humility have life to the full.

I hope you are starting to recognize the relationship between pride and idolatry. They first reared their ugly heads through Satan, and then through Adam and Eve, and from then on through every human being who has ever lived. In Ezekiel chapter 28 we are told of Satan's pride/idolatry. Satan, who was at first a guardian cherub, was not content in being who God created him to be and pride was found in his heart, and he said he was a god. Then Adam and Eve, in their pride/idolatry, listened to Satan, the king of pride and idolatry, and they wanted to be like God (Genesis 3:5). They thought they should determine what was good and evil.

Since the fall, every human being, including you and me, has tried to "play God" out of our pride. Please keep this in mind as we continue throughout this book. If you think you do not struggle in this way, you have just revealed your pride in failing to be honest.

When we are not convinced of what God says, we will not worship him. If we are not resting in his perfect love in Christ we will undoubtedly fall into idolatry. When we reject God and do not believe what he has said, we fall for a lie, and we come up empty.

I have seen many relational problems and fears in trials that could have been solved simply by being convinced of the promise of God that nothing in all of creation can separate us from the love of God in Christ (Romans 8:38, 39). I have seen this in my own life and in the lives of many people in many different situations. Not holding firmly to this promise affects our relationship with God, our relationships with others, and how we react to the circumstances of life. If only we were convinced!

For example, how many times when waiting on an answer to prayer have we refused to act in humility by trusting what God has said, resting in his love, and continuing to worship him? What do we do instead? In our pride we reject what God has said and we try to take things into our own hands. How many times have we done this? How many times have we regretted it? If we are honest and living according to truth, we have regretted it every time. Sometimes the consequences of pride are somewhat minor and sometimes they are major. Regardless of the consequences we experience, pride is always our enemy.

Another example of pride is how often we are unwilling to be submissive. This sin, like all others, is ultimately sin against God (Genesis 39:9). However, it can be played out in various ways in the different roles we fill in life. This happens when we, as individuals, are not submissive to God's Word (John

14:15), when wives are not submissive to their husbands (1 Peter 3:5-6), when children are not submissive to their parents (Colossians 3:20), when employees are not submissive to their employers (Colossians 3:22-24), when church members are not submissive to their elders (Hebrews 13:17), when citizens are not submissive to the governing authorities (Romans 13:1-7), and so on.

What will help us greatly to be motivated to be obedient to the Lord by being submissive? Simply this: being convinced that nothing can separate us from the love of God in Christ (Romans 8:38-39).

What is the result of being convinced? We will walk in humility and worship instead of pride and idolatry. We will love God and others. When we are convinced of God's love we will submit to him and to others in the God-given roles we are called to fulfill in life. Life goes more smoothly for everyone when we are obedient in being submissive in our God-ordained roles.

Disclaimer—obviously we are not to submit to others when they tell us to do what God forbids or not to do what he commands (Acts 5:29).

Please read the following verses and meditate on them:

"What, then, shall we say in response to this? If God is for us, who can be against us?...For I am *convinced* that neither death nor life, neither angels nor demons, neither the present nor the future, nor any powers, neither height nor depth, nor anything else in all creation, will be able to separate us from the love of God that is in Christ Jesus our Lord" (Romans 8:31, 38, 39, emphasis mine).

In these verses, Paul said that he was convinced that nothing could separate him from the love of God in Christ Jesus, and that if God was for him, no one could be against him. We, too, need to be convinced. These promises are for everyone in Christ. They are not just for the apostle Paul.

We know many things about Paul's life from the book of Acts and the epistles he wrote. Paul was a great man of God. He was bold and fearless. He feared God, not man. Yet we read that he was constantly pressing toward the goal (Philippians 3:14). Paul struggled with indwelling sin as we do (Romans 7:14-25). He was not perfect, but he found strength in his weaknesses.

We can be certain that Paul, at least to some degree, struggled with the two-sided coin of pride/idolatry like we do. We know that God, in his love, and as part of his perfect plan, gave Paul a thorn in his flesh to help keep him from pride. We read about this in 2 Corinthians 12:7-10:

> To keep me from becoming conceited because of these surpassing great revelations, there was given me a thorn in my flesh, a messenger of Satan, to torment me. Three times I pleaded with the Lord to take it away from me. But he said to me, 'My grace is sufficient for you, for my power is made perfect in weakness.' Therefore I will boast all the more gladly about my weaknesses, so that Christ's power may rest on me. That is why, for Christ's sake, I delight in weaknesses, in insults, in hardships, in persecutions, in difficulties. For when I am weak, then I am strong.

God, in his love, had given Paul this thorn in his flesh so that he would grow in his understanding of God's love. It sounds to me like Paul was convinced. Don't you agree? I mean, to be able to delight in the midst of weaknesses, insults, hardships, persecutions, and difficulties is not possible without being assured of God's love. Paul lived like he was convinced.

Paul was also bold. He knew that the "fear of man will prove to be a snare, but whoever trusts in the Lord is kept safe" (Proverbs 29:25). He did not worship human love and acceptance. If he received love from others, that was great; but if he did not, he knew that God loved him perfectly in Christ. Trusting in God's love for us in Christ will set us free from the trap of the fear of man.

We know from the book of Acts that Paul would stand up and share the gospel before anyone, including kings. He would also rebuke his fellow believers, even in public when necessary. In Galatians 2:11-21 Paul rebuked Peter in public (it may be helpful for you to read this passage). Paul was not trying to impress anyone. His concern was to please God. That is the way it should be. We who are in Christ should not be concerned with what people think of us, unless we are not loving God and others. We do not have to worship at the idol of the fear of man.

Please do not misunderstand my saying that we should not be concerned with what others think. We have balance in Scripture. We are not to be rude. We are to speak the truth in love and with gentleness and respect (Ephesians 4:15; 1 Peter 3:15). There are times to speak and times to be silent (Ecclesiastes 3:7). But when the time is right to confront someone as Paul did, the only opinion that really matters is God's. Paul was convinced of this as he rebuked Peter in Galatians chapter two.

People who are really concerned about living for God will want you to obey God by speaking the truth in love to them. They may not like it at first, but later they will thank you. Peter, and the whole church, was grateful that Paul rebuked Peter. What gave Paul the courage to do this? He feared God instead of man. He knew that God was the only one who could, and did, love him perfectly. Aren't you glad Paul was convinced? By God's grace, Paul was convinced that nothing could separate him from the love of God in Christ (Romans 8:39), and knowing this, he kept the truth of the gospel intact by rebuking Peter. Being convinced of God's love is what kept Paul from falling into idolatry, in the form of the fear of man, and bringing reproach to the gospel. Being convinced of God's love is what can keep us from falling into idolatry, in the form of the fear of man, and bringing reproach to the gospel.

Take some time to reflect on God's definition of love in 1 Corinthians 13:4-8:

> Love is patient, love is kind. It does not envy, it does not boast, it is not proud. It is not rude, it is not self-seeking, it is not easily angered, it keeps no record of wrongs. Love does not delight in evil but rejoices with the truth. It always protects, always trusts, always hopes, always perseveres. Love never fails.

If you are in Christ, how might your relationship with God and others change if you were convinced that God constantly loves you with the kind of love described in 1 Corinthians 13:4-8?

In the next chapter we will look more deeply into what it means to be in Christ. For only in Christ can we be convinced of this love.

Questions and Prayer

1. Do you understand the connection between pride and idolatry? If you are not sure, and cannot explain it to someone else, go back and slowly read the chapter again. Explain this principle to someone else to help both you, and him, understand it more deeply.

2. How can being convinced of God's love help free you from your struggle with pride and idolatry? Write out specific thoughts to help you process this idea and then explain it to someone else.

3. In what areas in your life do you need to put off pride and idolatry and put on humility and worship? Write down specific areas. When these thoughts or situations occur in your life, meditate on how to rest and walk in God's love. Be preventative.

4. Pray that God will show you the pride and idolatry in your heart, and that he will turn them into humility and worship through a deeper conviction of the depth of his love for you in Christ.

Chapter 3

In Christ

"For I am convinced that neither death nor life, neither angels nor demons, neither the present nor the future, nor any powers, neither height nor depth, nor anything else in all creation, will be able to separate us from the love of God that is *in Christ* Jesus our Lord" (Romans 8:38-39, emphasis mine).

The verses above make it clear that the promise that nothing can separate us from the love of God is only true for those who are in Christ. Therefore, this promise is conditioned upon being in Christ. But what does it mean to be "in Christ" and how does one get "in Christ"?

In Christ

Paul used the phrase, "in Christ," with variants such as, "in him," approximately 160 times in the New Testament. From God's perspective, there are only two kinds of people in this world when we consider where a person is spiritually. There are those who are "in Christ" and those who are "in Adam." Those "in Christ" are spiritually alive. Those "in

Adam" are spiritually dead. There is no middle ground between these two groups of people. It is impossible to be partly "in Christ" and partly "in Adam." There are many distinctions in life in which we can fall into only one of two categories. For example, when we give personal information, we are often asked to give our marital status and sex. There is no middle ground in these categories. You are either married or you're not. You are either male or you're female. So it is with being "in Christ" or "in Adam." You are either in one or the other.

We will look at what it means to be "in Adam," and how one gets "in Adam," after we look at what it means to be "in Christ" and how one gets "in Christ."

Those who are in Christ are eternally united to Christ. They are no longer spiritually dead in their sins and separated from Christ. They have come into relationship with him through the regenerating work of the Holy Spirit, who has given them spiritual life (John 3:3-8; Ephesians 2:4, 5). As a result of being given spiritual life, those in Christ respond in repentance toward God and faith in the Lord Jesus (Acts 11:18; 16:14; 20:21).

John Murray writes, "Union with Christ is the central truth of the whole doctrine of salvation."[5] Those who are in Christ have all the promises of all the spiritual riches in Christ. They are spiritually alive (regenerated/born again), they are new creations, they have been given faith and repentance, they have been declared righteous, their sins have been forgiven, they have Jesus' perfect life (his righteousness) credited to their account, they have been adopted into God's family, they have the promise that God will complete the work he began in them, they have all the promises of God in Christ, they are

---

[5] John Murray, *Redemption Accomplished and Applied* (Grand Rapids, MI: Wm. B. Eerdmans Publishing Company, 1955), 170.

perfectly loved by God, and they have the promise of life everlasting in the presence of God in a resurrected and glorified body in which they will never sin again. Let's look at just a few of the promises to those who are in Christ, but I urge you to search the Bible for yourself, and you will find many more:

> Praise be to the God and Father of our Lord Jesus Christ, who has blessed us in the heavenly realms with every spiritual blessing *in Christ* (Ephesians 1:3, emphasis mine).
>
> Therefore, if anyone is *in Christ*, he is a new creation; the old has gone, and the new has come! (2 Corinthians 5:17, emphasis mine).
>
> God made him who had no sin to be sin for us, so that *in him* we might become the righteousness of God (2 Corinthians 5:21, emphasis mine).
>
> And you also were included *in Christ* when you heard the word of truth, the gospel of your salvation. Having believed, you were marked *in him* with a seal, the promised Holy Spirit, who is a deposit guaranteeing our inheritance until the redemption of those who are God's possession—to the praise of his glory (Ephesians 1:13-14, emphasis mine).
>
> For as *in Adam* all die, so *in Christ* all will be made alive (1 Corinthians 15:22, emphasis mine).

> Be kind and compassionate to one another, forgiving each other just as *in Christ* God forgave you (Ephesians 4:32, emphasis mine).

> For I am convinced that neither life nor death, neither angels nor demons, neither the present nor the future, nor any powers, neither height nor depth, nor anything else in all creation will be able to separate us from the love of God that is *in Christ* Jesus our Lord (Romans 8:38-39, emphasis mine).

According to God's Word, only those in Christ can be convinced that nothing can separate them from God's perfect love. This is possible only because of the person and work of Christ. Jesus is fully God and fully man. He lived a sinless life. After living a perfect life, he died on the cross to pay the sin debt in full for those who believe in him. Then, after being buried, he was raised from the dead on the third day to give them life, so they can be eternally united to him.

How does someone get in Christ? From the viewpoint of eternity past, God chose the elect in Christ before the creation of the world (Ephesians 1:4-6; 2 Timothy 1:9). However, someone is not actually in Christ until God gives him spiritual life (Romans 8:30; 2 Thessalonians 2:13). When a person is given spiritual life, he responds in repentance and faith. These gifts are given to us by God and yet we must exercise them. We must repent and believe. God does not repent and believe for us. A person who has been given spiritual life desires to turn from his sin to God with full intention of living an obedient life (he repents), and trusts Jesus' death on the cross as full payment for his sins and Jesus' resurrection as his only hope of eternal life. He receives the free gift of eternal life and Jesus as his Lord and Savior.

Can a person in Christ doubt God's love? We who are in Christ can struggle with being convinced that nothing can separate us from the love of God in Christ Jesus our Lord (Romans 8:39). We can go through periods of doubt, especially in difficult circumstances, wondering whether God is good and if he is for us (Romans 8:28, 31). We can also struggle with being convinced that we are accepted in Christ (Romans 15:7). None of us is perfectly convinced all the time.

The good news is that the apostle Paul tells us in the book of Romans that we can be convinced. Paul was not beyond falling victim to pride and idolatry himself. Though he failed at times, he knew that he was perfectly loved in Christ; and that made an amazing difference in his relationship with God and with others. Being convinced of this truth can rescue us from many temptations to think, say, and do things that are contrary to God's will.

If you are in Christ, I hope and pray that you will become increasingly convinced of God's holy and perfect love.

In Adam

Now what about the only other kind of people who exist from God's perspective? I am speaking of those in Adam. Those who are in Adam are not forgiven of any of their sins, do not have eternal life, are seen as unholy, have no righteousness, are spiritually dead, possess none of the spiritual riches in Christ, have none of the good promises of God, are separated from the perfect love of God in Christ, are hell-bound, and are children of the devil. I could go on but I will let you search the Bible, and you will see all the things God says about those who are in Adam.

How do people get in Adam? They do not have to do anything. They just have to be born into this world of two sinful parents, which all of us are. We stand guilty because Adam's sin, and the effects of original sin, have been passed down through procreation to the whole human race ever since Adam, our representative, fell (Psalm 51:5; Romans 5:12-19). If a person does not become united to Christ, he continues in Adam.

Some people who are in Adam think that somehow their good will outweigh their bad. Some think they are good, or at least better than other people that they know. Some are atheist, some are agnostic, and some do not really care at all. Some are religious. Some believe in God. Some are members of a cult. Some are members of non-Christian religions. Some are members of Christian denominations. Some have prayed "the prayer." Some have been baptized. Some even believe in Jesus, but only on an intellectual and/or emotional level, without true saving faith. But all of these people are in Adam, separate from eternal life, separate from forgiveness, and separate from the perfect love of God that can only be found only in Christ.

Some people think that God loves them and accepts them just as they are, even though they are not in Christ. I hope you are not one who believes this. If you do, you have created a "god" to your own liking. In reality, the God who created you is holy, and he is just, or he would not be God at all. If you have not trusted Christ's death as full payment for your sins, you will spend all eternity in conscious torment in hell.

Would you consider a human judge to be just if he simply let people off the hook for breaking the law? Certainly not! So, how can anyone imagine that God, who is holy and just, will simply let people off for breaking his law? The only way to escape his wrath is to be in Christ.

If You Are Not in Christ, Do You Want to Be?

To be in Christ means that you are in a relationship with Christ based on his word. I need to make a cautionary statement here because I have heard people say that they have their "own thing" going with God. They say they have a "personal relationship" with God. Let me make it quite clear that to have a personal relationship with God comes on his terms, not ours. It is his thing, not our thing. It comes only through Jesus, and by way of saving faith and genuine repentance.

If you are not in Christ, please continue to examine the claims of this book according to the Bible. I want you to know the perfect love of God in Christ. You cannot genuinely know God's love until you repent and believe.

Biblical Balance

I must say a few words to hopefully preclude any misunderstandings of what I mean by someone in Christ being perfectly loved by God. If someone is in Christ, God does and will forever perfectly love him as his child covered in the righteousness of Christ. This does not mean, however, that God loves everything a person in Christ does. God is holy and he is love so he hates sin. He will always hate sin. He hates what hurts our relationship with him, what hurts others, and what hurts us. Because he loves us, we have the promise that God will lovingly discipline those who are his:

> My son, do not make light of the Lord's discipline, and do not lose heart when he rebukes you, because the Lord disciplines those he loves, and he punishes everyone he accepts as a son (Hebrews 12:5, 6).

Scripture warns us to work out our salvation with fear and trembling (Philippians 2:12). We should fear displeasing the God who loves us perfectly. We are to properly fear God, which shows itself in our obedience to him. We should be in awe of him; for he is holy. A biblical fear of God does not mean that we should be afraid that he is going to harm us. God is always for us according to his holy will, and nothing can separate us from his love in Christ (Romans 8:31, 38-39). Psalm 33:18 says, "But the eyes of the Lord are on those who fear him, on those whose hope is in his unfailing love." In this verse we see that those who hope in God's love fear him and those who fear him hope in his love. You cannot separate biblical fear of God from biblical hope in his love. When you are convinced of the perfect, unending, unfailing, steadfast love of God in Christ you will properly fear God and thus trust and obey him. And when you biblically fear God you will be convinced of the perfect, unending, unfailing, steadfast love of God in Christ and thus trust and obey him. You cannot separate God's holiness from his love and you cannot separate his love from his holiness.

May we never forget that the Bible motivates us toward obedience by teaching us that we will all stand before the judgment seat of Christ for an appraisal of what we have done in the body (2 Corinthians 5:9-10). Do we not want to hear "well done, good and faithful servant" from the one who loves us perfectly in Christ?

Many people have a hard time separating our secure and eternal standing or position in Christ from what we do. We need to understand this distinction. For example, when we cannot take reproof for our actions in a godly way, we think, say, and do things that are unacceptable to God. I am sure there have been times when all of us have been rebuked, and instead of having truly sought change out of love for God, we responded in anger. We became mean and unforgiving. This is a double-edged sword for the proud person who fears man. We want people to love and accept us, yet instead of seeking change we get angry, which usually causes more rejection. This is serious bondage. It is pride feeding the fear of man, and the fear of man feeding pride. If we are convinced of God's perfect love for us in Christ, we can accept reproof and grow because of it. We can actually come to welcome it when we are convinced of his love.

On the other hand, there may be times when we do not accept reproof, and do not seek any change, simply out of pride which is not mixed with the fear of man. We may not really fear rejection from people that much. We just do not want to change. This, too, is pride. The perfect love of God in Christ can humble and motivate us to see our sin as it really is, and teach us to grow toward Christ-likeness and thus change for the glory of God. We need to become convinced of God's love!

In either of the above two examples we are acting stupidly according to God. Proverbs 12:1 says, "Whoever loves discipline loves knowledge, but he who hates correction is stupid."

All of God's commandments are summed up in the commands to love him with all of our heart, soul, mind, and strength, and to love our neighbor as ourselves (Matthew 22:37-39). Sin is always unloving. As we saw in Hebrews 12, God will lovingly discipline those who are in Christ in the way he sees fit. This does not, however, change what God thinks of us as his children. If we are in Christ, we are seen as perfect in his sight because of what Jesus has done. This never changes.

Avoiding God's discipline, working out our salvation with fear and trembling, standing before the judgment seat of Christ, pleasing God, and living for his glory are all biblical motives for obedience in the Christian life. Actually, all of these motives are intertwined together. They are all connected and interrelated to some degree. And they are also connected and interrelated with another biblical motivation that we see repeated over and over throughout Scripture. This motivation for trusting and obeying God is the love, grace, and mercy of God that we have in being united to Christ. "The fact of union with Christ in his death to sin and new life to God is the foundation for growth in holiness; the knowledge of it provides the motivation."[6] According to the Bible, no one who is truly in Christ will proudly, continually, and willfully remain in sin. "No one who is born of God will continue to sin, because God's seed remains in him; he cannot go on sinning, because he has been born of God" (1 John 3:9).

Those of us in Christ will continue to struggle with sin, but we will not comfortably remain in it. When we do sin, we are to confess our sins to the God who loves us perfectly. We are to agree with him that what we have done is first and foremost sin against him, and then sin against others, if, in fact, we have sinned against others. We are to seek forgiveness from God and others. We must repent and ask God to help us to walk in obedience. We need to be disciplined concerning the use of the means of spiritual growth. The means of spiritual growth include corporate worship, biblically sound preaching and teaching, biblical counseling, prayer, baptism, communion/Lord's Supper, fasting, personal Bible study and prayer, Scripture memorization, family worship, generous giving, fellowship, evangelism, accountability, confession of sin, informal and formal peacemaking/church discipline, serving with our spiritual gifts and talents, etc.

It is the grace of God that teaches us to say no to ungodliness:

---

[6] Sinclair B. Ferguson, *The Holy Spirit: Contours of Christian Theology* (Downers Grove, IL: Inter Varsity Press, 1996), 152.

For the grace of God that brings salvation has appeared to all men. It teaches us to say "No" to ungodliness and worldly passions, and to live self-controlled, upright and godly lives in this present age, while we wait for the blessed hope—the glorious appearing of our great God and Savior, Jesus Christ, who gave himself for us to redeem us from all wickedness and to purify for himself a people that are his very own, eager to do what is good (Titus 2:11-14).

God wants all of us to become convinced of his grace, and the fact that if we are in Christ we are perfectly loved. Being convinced of this will compel us to trust and obey him in every area of our life:

For Christ's love compels us, because we are convinced that one died for all, and therefore all died. And he died for all, that those who live should no longer live for themselves but for him who died for them and was raised again (2 Corinthians 5:14-15).

I want to end this chapter with the beloved passage from Romans 8:28-39. Please meditate on these verses and what they say to you who are in Christ.

And we know that in all things God works for the good of those who love him, who have been called according to his purpose. For those God foreknew he also predestined to be conformed to the likeness of his Son, that he might be the firstborn among many brothers. And those he predestined, he also called; those he called, he also justified; those he justified, he also glorified. What, then, shall we say in response to this? If God is for us, who can be against us? He who did not spare his own Son, but gave him up for us all—how will he not also, along with him, graciously give us all things? Who will bring any charge against those whom God has chosen? It is God who justifies. Who is he that condemns? Christ Jesus, who died—more than that, who was raised to life—is at the right hand of God and is also interceding for us. Who shall separate us from the love of Christ? Shall trouble or hardship or persecution or famine or nakedness or danger or sword? As it is written: "For your sake we face death all day long; we are considered as sheep to be slaughtered." No, in all these things we are more than conquerors through him who loved us. For I am convinced that neither death nor life, neither angels nor demons, neither the present nor the future, nor any powers, neither height nor depth, nor anything else in all creation, will be able to separate us from the love of God that is *in Christ Jesus* our Lord (Romans 8:28-39, emphasis mine).

Questions and Prayer

1. Are you in Christ? If not, and you desire to be, call upon the name of the Lord. Confess to him that you have sinned against him knowing that you deserve nothing but his judgment and wrath. Repent—be willing to turn from all sin with God's help—as you receive Christ as your Lord and Savior. Believe that Jesus is fully God and fully man. Trust in Jesus' death on the cross as full payment for your sins. Trust in his resurrection as your only hope of eternal life. Pray daily for God to make you more like Christ as you submit to his word.

2. Are you able to clearly see a healthy distinction between your standing in Christ and what you do? Seek balance in this area and trust what God says rather than your feelings.

3. What motivates you toward obedience? Are your motives biblically balanced? Pray for God to reveal your heart concerning this.

Chapter 4

What You Do or Your Standing?

Does knowing that nothing can separate you from the love of God in Christ Jesus (Romans 8:38-39) lead to pride and idolatry or humility and worship? If you have a biblical view of God and a biblical view of yourself the answer is obvious. It leads to humility and worship. A biblical view of God sees God as awesome, holy, loving, and the greatest treasure known to man. A biblical view of man sees ourselves as completely unworthy of God's love, utterly dependent upon God for salvation and daily living, and yet perfectly loved by God if we are in Christ. Does this promise not encourage you to trust and obey God in everything? Does not knowing that you are always loved with the kind of love described in 1 Corinthians 13:4-8 lead you to humility and worship? Once again, if you have a biblical view of God and a biblical view of yourself the answer is obviously yes. Notice I said that we are "always" loved by God in Christ. God is love (1 John 4:8). He is unchanging. His character never changes. It is impossible for him to be unloving at any time. Not even for one second does God cease being love. No one else fits this description. No person in the history of the world has fit this description for even a single day. The only exception, of course, is Jesus, who is not just fully man, but also fully God, and therefore loves perfectly.

Let us remember that God defines love not merely as a feeling or emotion. God's kind of love involves choice and action. Immediately after the Bible tells us "God is love" in 1 John 4:8, we read, "This is how God showed his love among us: He sent his one and only Son into the world that we might live through him. This is love: not that we loved God, but that he loved us and sent his Son as an atoning sacrifice for our sins" (1 John 4:9-11). Here we see God's love shown in choice and action: God sent his Son. It is sacrificial: his Son was sent as a sacrifice. It is unfailing: it was not in response to our love for God.

God's love is also not irresponsibly permissive. He does not delight in evil but rejoices with the truth (1 Corinthians 13:6). God hates sin. Love hates sin. God's kind of love hates the sin people commit, and yet loves the person who commits it. Likewise, we must also understand the difference between hating the sin of others and yet still loving them.

Hate Sin; Love People

As Christians, we should love all people but we should hate their sin. This should be the case even with our spouses and children. Why? God loves people and yet he hates sin. Jesus had to die for sin. Sin hurts our relationship with God, and sin hurts people. "Love must be sincere. Hate what is evil; cling to what is good" (Romans 12:9).

Let me give you an example by using the sin of homosexuality. True biblical Christianity will always hate the sin of homosexuality, yet, at the same time, will love people living in this lifestyle, help them in any way that is good for them, share the gospel with them, and pray for them to repent. This should be true of anyone caught in any sin. We also hate gossip and gluttony, or at least we should.

Are All Sins Equal?

Please do not misunderstand me. I am not saying that homosexuality, adultery, premarital sex, or any sexual sin is on the same level as a lesser sin like unhealthy worry. The Bible teaches very clearly that there are different degrees of sin. Some sins are worse than others, but God hates all sin, and so should we, especially our own.

You may have heard someone use the statement "sin is sin." Using this statement is an example of where we need to explain ourselves very clearly and define the meaning that we are pouring into our words. If, when we say, "sin is sin," we mean that no matter what sin we have committed (without trusting Jesus' death on the cross as full payment, and his resurrection as our only hope of eternal life), we justly deserve to spend eternity in hell, then yes, "sin is sin." The Bible teaches that "the wages of *sin* is death but the gift of God is eternal life in Christ Jesus Our Lord" (Romans 6:23, emphasis mine). All sin, no matter how small or big, deserves eternal hell. But to say that some sins are no worse than others is just plain false. As Anthony Hoekema writes, "All forms of sin are displeasing to God and entail guilt. Not every sin, however, is equally serious."[7] Jesus, said to Pilate, "Therefore the one who handed me over to you is guilty of a *greater* sin" (John 19:11, emphasis mine). Since Jesus, who is God, said that some sins are greater than others, then obviously there are some sins that are greater than others.

---

[7] Anthony A. Hoekema, *Created in God's Image* (Grand Rapids, MI: William B. Eerdmans Publishing Company, 1986), 177.

If some sins were not judged as worse than others we would have an unjust God. Can you imagine a human judge, let alone a just God, who would equate speeding and murder as equal crimes? Speeding and murder are both breaking the law, but are they on an equal level as to the degree of their severity? Maybe, if you live on Mars. God is just and there are different degrees of sin. Because God is just there are also different degrees of reward in heaven and different degrees of punishment in hell (Luke 12:47-48; 1 Corinthians 3:10-15; 2 Corinthians 5:10).

So we can say that "sin is sin" only in the sense that all sin deserves eternal separation from God. Knowing this should remove pride and self-righteousness from our lives because we all have sinned. I think one of the reasons people use the saying "sin is sin" is to try to stop people from being self-righteous. If this is the reason, the motive is good; but we must be as biblically accurate as possible and explain ourselves as clearly as possible to try to prevent people from misunderstanding. Maybe it would be wisest to not use this statement at all. We can teach both the truth that all sin deserves hell, and that there are different degrees of sin, without saying "sin is sin."

By God's common grace, even those outside of Christ understand that the sin of murder and the sin of unhealthy worry are not equal in degree. The problem is that they will not accept the truth that both deserve eternal hell.

The good news is that God's love for you who are in Christ is not based on what you do, but in what God has done for you in Christ. Christ has taken away our sins and he has credited his righteousness to our account. Aren't you glad? If his love was based on what we do, we would have no hope. We must understand the difference between our standing or position in Christ, and what we do. As Christians, we are to grieve over our sin and turn from it. But we are also to rejoice in our standing in Christ (1 John 3:1). We are beloved people in Christ. This balance keeps us from both an unhealthy wallowing in guilt after we repented, confessed and dealt with our sin, and from thinking that we now have a license to sin.

As a word of caution, we must remember that our rejoicing in our standing in Christ must be a rejoicing in God and what he has done for us in Christ. We are not to rejoice in ourselves. Our thoughts are to be directed on how great God is, not how great we are. Focusing on ourselves leads us to pride and idolatry rather than humility and worshipping God.

Remember Your Standing in Christ

When those of us in Christ are not resting in the perfect love of God and our eternal and secure standing in Christ we turn to idolatry. Setting aside who God has made us in his Son often leads to the unbiblical behaviors tied to whoever we think we are at the time. We often act out who we think we are or who others tell us we are.

When we are not resting in our secure standing in Christ, we look elsewhere. This often plays out with people defining themselves by just about anything imaginable. For example, people label themselves by their occupation, outward appearance, hobbies, talents, family, financial position, etc. We often try to attach ourselves to anything in search of an "identity."

As you may have noticed I am using quotation marks around the word "identity" to highlight the pervasive baggage that is often associated with this word as it relates to the field of psychology and psychological thinking both in our culture and its influence in the church.

God does clearly tell those of us in Christ who we are in him. We are the light of the world (Matthew 5:14). We are his sheep (Matthew 25:32). We are the elect (Mark 13:20). We are alive and found (Luke 15:24). We are children of God (John 1:12-13). We are believers (Acts 2:44). We are slaves to God (Romans 6:22). We are wretched men who need daily rescue from the power of sin through Jesus Christ (Romans 7:24-25). We are not our own; we were bought at a price (1 Corinthians 6:19-20). We are new creations in Christ (2 Corinthians 5:17). We are sons of God (Galatians 3:26). We are children of light (Ephesians 5:8). We are saints (Philippians 1:1). We are God's chosen people, holy and dearly loved (Colossians 3:12). We are brothers loved by God (1 Thessalonians 1:4). We are God's household (1 Timothy 3:15). We are the Lord's servants (2 Timothy 2:24). We are a people that are God's very own (Titus 2:14). We are Jesus' brothers (Hebrews 2:11). We are chosen (James 2:5). We are a royal priesthood and a holy nation (1 Peter 2:9). We are perfectly loved children of God (1 John 3:1). We are a kingdom and priests (Revelation 1:6).

This is just a limited description of who God says we are in Christ. There are many more verses in both the New and Old Testaments describing believers. If you take the time to look up these verses and any others describing who God says we are, you will find that God tells us who we are for the purpose of our seeing how great he is (for he has made us who we are) and also as a motivation to our trusting and obeying him. God does not tell us who we are in Christ so that we will think great things about ourselves. He tells us who we are so that we will think great things about who he is and what he has done for us in Christ. The vast number of verses telling us who we are in Christ makes it obvious that God thinks it is important for us to know who we are in him. And when we look at the context of these verses we will see his purpose in doing so. His purpose is to lead us to humility and worship, not pride and idolatry.

Recently, a friend of mine was asked by someone who had not seen him in quite some time what he was now doing in life. He responded by defining himself by his occupation. How will my friend define himself if his occupation becomes obsolete? What if he becomes unable to perform his job? What happens to a person who has his whole "identity" wrapped up in his occupation if, for one reason or another, he is no longer able to work in that occupation? He will be devastated.

All of us are going to age and our looks will change. We will have serious pride, idolatry, and fear of man issues when we look in the mirror, not liking what we see, if our "identity" is wrapped up in our appearance.

For example, before I became a Christian I worshipped the way I looked. I had very long, thick, and (as I was often told) attractive hair. I worked out a lot and would lie out in the sun for hours to maintain a dark tan. I wore sleeveless shirts constantly, even during the winter, to show off my biceps. My whole "identity" was wrapped up in my appearance. By following my own deceitful heart, being influenced by the people around me, and listening to the world, I had bought into the lie that outward appearance is "where it is at." This lie says that if you look great, and people think you look great, you will be happy. Thank God the truth set me free from this lie. I can remember back to before I became a Christian, when my hair first started to fall out, and the fear that came with it. Then, by God's grace, I became a Christian, and very early in my Christian walk I became secure in my standing in Christ. To my amazement, all my hair is gone now and it does not bother me. If, however, I was not secure in my standing in Christ, I know that I would be miserable. I still work out today, on a much smaller scale, to stay in shape so I can serve God and others, but my motive has changed. Now I work out to be a good steward of the body God has given me rather than, in my pride and fear of man, trying to impress people.

For others, their "identity" is wrapped up in their hobbies. Yet they may change hobbies or become unable to enjoy them. What are you going to do if your "identity" is wrapped up in these things, and you can no longer enjoy them? You may someday become too sick to use many of your talents.

For those who cling too tightly to family members and find their "identity" in those relationships, what are you going to do if those relationships change? You may lose your spouse or children. Your family situation may change in a number of ways.

Others have their "identity" in their financial position and material possessions, which we all know can change overnight. You cannot take anything with you when you die. However, your standing in Christ will last forever.

Change in life can be hard for any of us. It can be very difficult at times. However, if we are resting in our standing in Christ, we can experience the peace and joy of God even in painful circumstances. I recently lost someone very dear to me who encouraged me throughout life, including in the writing of this book. I can say to you that though this has been a difficult time I have experienced the supernatural peace and joy of God in the midst of this loss. This has been the case only because, by God's grace, I have been resting in my standing in Christ, and have remained convinced of his love for me.

I previously listed many different descriptions of who we are in Christ. Yet, when you look closely at all of these you will see that they are all interrelated and are all different ways of describing who we are in Christ. I am now going to focus on one of those descriptions, but please keep in mind that all of the ways God describes his people are included in this one description. And please remember that God tells us who we are for his glory, not ours, and so that we will be motivated to live for him.

If we are in Christ, the Bible says we are children of God. That is the only standing that can never change and is eternal. Those who have become children of God will always be children of God. This standing is sufficient, or at least it should be.

Why would I try to attach an "identity" to myself when I have the standing I have in Christ? If I am in Christ, my standing is secure for eternity. My standing is who God says I am. That should be good enough. This truth reminds me of the time the disciples went out preaching and were casting out demons. With great excitement they came back to tell Jesus what they had done, and he said, "Rejoice that your names are written in heaven" (Luke 10:20). In other words, Jesus was teaching them to rejoice in who they were and not in what they had done. The joy of what happens today will soon fade, but the joy of who God is and what he has done for you in Christ will never fade. It will last forever. It will never change. It is secure. And guess what—we will be secure when we are convinced of who we are in Christ and the blessings that come with it.

To preclude any misunderstanding concerning our standing in Christ, I want to say that we all have many roles to fill in life, and we do many things that are important. We are all tied to many different relationships. I have a role to play as a husband, a father, a son, a brother, a friend, an employee, an elder, a guitar player, a writer, and so on. Yet I do not want to put my ultimate standing in these roles. I am, first and foremost, a child of God, who is related to many different people in my sphere of relationships and who has been gifted by God to do certain things. If all of my relationships were to change, and if I could no longer do what I am now able to do, I would still be a child of God. It is much wiser, if you are in Christ, to see yourself as whom God says you are instead of labeling yourself by what you do and by the roles you fill. When I am focused on how great God is and what he has done for me in Christ I will fulfill my roles in humility and worship to him out of my standing in Christ rather than placing my hope in some "identity" in my pride and idolatry.

Using the words written by the apostle John, let's look a little deeper into what the standing of being a child of God really means. "How great is the love the Father has lavished on us, that we should be called children of God. And that is what we are! The reason the world does not know us is that it did not know him" (1 John 3:1). If you are in Christ, God says that you are a child of God. He says that is who you are. This standing is based on who you are in Christ.

I want to expose an error in the minds of many people. We must understand that no one is a child of God unless he is in Christ. You hear people say things like, "We are all just God's children," meaning that all human beings are children of God. Few statements are as unbiblical as this one. The Bible is very clear that God created all of mankind, but the Bible is also very clear that only those who have been born again, born from above, are children of God. Everyone who has not been born again is a child of the devil. Having said this, let us never forget that even those of us who are born again would still be living in a state of total depravity if God had not adopted us into his family. If it were not for God choosing to bring us from darkness to light through the new birth, we would still be children of the devil.

If you have a problem with the fact that not everyone is a child of God, let's look at what the Bible says:

Yet to all who received him, to those who believed in his name, he gave the right to become children of God—children born not of natural descent, nor of human decision or a husband's will, but born of God (John 1:12-13).

It is clear from these verses in the gospel of John, as well as verses in First John and many other places in the Bible, that only those in Christ are children of God.

Many people, trying to suit their own needs, have created a "god" in their own minds who does not even exist. How many people do you know who do not claim to be in Christ, and yet they talk about the love of God, or quote that God is love? Or when talking of God, they refer to the "good lord," as in the "good lord this" or the "good lord that?"

The God of the Bible is a holy God. Yes, God is love and he is always good, but he is also always holy. Love hates sin. Sin destroys people. The God of the Bible, who created everyone, will pour out his wrath for eternity on those who have not been adopted into his family.

Those of us in Christ know that God is holy. Knowing that God is holy is what makes his love for us so amazing. If he were not holy there would be no need of true love, there would be no need of grace, and there would be no need of mercy. There would be no perfect love if God were not holy. That is why John writes, "How great is the love the Father has lavished on us. That we should be called children of God!" (1 John 3:1).

The "us" and the "we" spoken of here by John refer to those in Christ. What is so great about this love? The answer is that we are wretched and evil. That is why God's love is so great. That is why it is, and has to be, perfect.

The Bible does not shy away from telling us who we are apart from Christ. Take a moment to look at just a few of these statements in Scripture:

"Everyone has turned away, they have together become corrupt; there is no one who does good, not even one" (Psalm 53:3).

"All of us have become like one who is unclean, and all our righteous acts are like filthy rags" (Isaiah 64:6).

"The heart is deceitful above all things and beyond cure. Who can understand it?" (Jeremiah 17:9).

Jesus speaking to his disciples said, "If you, then, though you are *evil*, know how to give good gifts to your children, how much more will your Father in heaven give good gifts to those who ask him!" (Matthew 7:11, emphasis mine).

"For all have sinned and fallen short of the glory of God" (Romans 3:23).

The apostle Paul said, "What a wretched man I am! Who will rescue me from this body of death?" (Romans 7:24).

This is just a small taste of what the Bible says about us apart from Christ. What we hear in our culture is often in direct opposition to the word of God. The culture often tells us that we are "basically good," "our good will outweigh our bad," or "I'm okay, you're okay." We often hear things like "you're just a victim" or "it is not really your fault."

The point is that when many people talk about God loving them, or his being love, they have not even looked to the Bible for their understanding of who God is or what love is. They are talking about a "god" they have created, not the God who created them. Many people say, "God loves me and accepts me unconditionally," yet they have no understanding of what that means so it has no real affect on their lives.

Until a person sees the seriousness of his sin, which can happen only if the Holy Spirit shows him, he will never know God, nor will he ever understand or know his love. "When he comes, he will convict the world of guilt in regard to sin and righteousness and judgment" (John 16:8). "The man without the Spirit does not accept the things from the Spirit of God, for they are foolishness to him, and he cannot understand them, because they are spiritually discerned" (1 Corinthians 2:14).

Being convinced of God's perfect love in Christ really means nothing to a person until he is born again by the Spirit of God. This love never reaches our hearts until the Holy Spirit regenerates us. There is no reality to it until then.

Let's look at 1 John 3:1 again:

> How great is the love the Father has lavished on us that we should be called children of God! And that is what we are! The reason the world does not know us is that it did not know him.

What an amazing verse! You can almost feel the passion and excitement that John must have experienced when he wrote this verse under the inspiration of the Holy Spirit. John knows that God's love is great because he has lavished his love on evil, wicked, undeserving people like John, who deserve nothing but eternal hell, and he has chosen them and now calls them children of God. The "we" here refers to people who know they do not deserve God's love. They know they deserve only his wrath. That is why God's love is so great to them. That is why it makes a radical difference in their lives. That is why the only standing that matters is that of being a child of God. John speaks in amazement here. It is as if he were saying, "It is too good to be true that we should be called children of God." Yet that is what God says we are if we are in Christ. How can we improve on that? Why would we want to? God loves me and accepts me into his family, so why do I "need" to look elsewhere? Why commit idolatry and spiritual adultery against God by searching for a "label" outside of who we are in Christ?

This verse also teaches us that the world does not understand those who are children of God. It cannot understand because it does not know God. No one can know God until, through the work of the Holy Spirit, he sees himself as a wretched sinner. Then he must turn to the only remedy, Jesus' death and resurrection. It is in Jesus' death that our sins are removed. It is in his resurrection that his life is given to us and his perfection is credited to our account. The world cannot understand the things of God unless they are regenerated.

Many people think they are children of God regardless of whether they are in Christ or not. They think they can earn or deserve heaven. They think they can earn or deserve God's love. With that kind of thinking, God's love doesn't mean much at all. Humans love like that.

It is easy to see why those who are not in Christ turn to false gods—people, places, and things—trying to "find something." They do not know God. They do not have or know his undeserved love. To them, being a child of God is really not that amazing. Many people even think God owes them something.

But those of us in Christ know that being called a child of God is the greatest and most undeserved gift in the world. We know we are wretched. We know we have been saved from eternal conscious torment in hell. That is why we can say with John, "How great is the love that the Father has lavished on us, that we should be called children of God! And that is what we are!" (1 John 3:1).

Who are you? If you are in Christ, you have been undeservingly adopted into the family of God. You are perfectly loved by God. You have been blessed with every spiritual blessing in Christ. By God's grace, you have become a child of God, and that is what will motivate you to glorify God in everything you do and every circumstance you find yourself in. This is exactly what Paul teaches us in Ephesians 5 verse 8, "For you were once darkness, but now you are light in the Lord. Live as children of light." He says the same thing in 1 Thessalonians 5 verse 5, "You are all sons of the light and sons of the day. We do not belong to the night or to the darkness." In other words, Paul teaches us to go be who we are. It makes no sense for children of light to live in darkness. However, it makes all the sense in the world for children of God to live for their Father's glory.

Questions and Prayer

1. If someone were to ask you who you are, how would you respond?

2. In whom, what, or where have you been "finding" your "identity"? Do you see the dangers in doing this?

3. Do you understand how freeing it is to rest in your standing in Christ, rather than in what you do?

4. Do you see how resting in who you are in Christ can lead to a greater resting in God's love, and therefore, to greater obedience to him? Ask God to help you with this.

5. Write out and explain to someone how God perfectly loves those who are in Christ and yet does not love or accept their sin. If you need help with this, ask your pastor/elder.

6. Pray that God will show you the depths of your sin and how truly hopeless you are apart from Christ, and yet, at the same time, how perfect you are in God's sight through Christ. When you come to a deep grasp of these two truths, you will be humbled and bow in worship.

Chapter 5

Live for God's Glory!

Are you resting in the great love the Father has lavished on you in Christ? Are you convinced? Are you heading in that direction? I pray that all of us in Christ are. So far we have laid the solid foundation that if we are in Christ we are perfectly loved by God. We know we do not deserve this love and that is what makes it so amazing. The standing given to those in Christ is amazing as well. We are children of God and "that is what we are" (1 John 3:1). It is foolish for those in Christ to search for an "identity" or label ourselves. We have an eternal standing in Christ. It is foolish for us to worship and serve the creation in a futile effort to find fulfillment. Our pride/idolatry struggle is put to rest when we are convinced that God loves us perfectly in Christ.

I need to make another cautionary statement at this time. Our desire for fulfillment is certainly not priority number one in life. Our number one priority and desire in life should be to love God (Mathew 22:37-38). Priority number one is the glory of God. We are to live for God's glory. Life is about trusting and obeying God. Glorifying God is the purpose of our existence.

We were created by and for God (Colossians 1:16). He does not exist for us. Our focus should, first and foremost, be on God and not on our own desires. It is true, however, that when our focus is on the things of God, he will be glorified, and we will be satisfied. John Piper, Pastor for Preaching at Bethlehem Baptist Church in Minneapolis, Minnesota writes, "God is most glorified in us when we are most satisfied in him."[8]

Jesus told the woman at the well, "If you knew the gift of God and who it is that asks you for a drink, you would have asked him and he would have given you living water" (John 4:10). Then Jesus went on to say, "Everyone who drinks this water will be thirsty again, but whoever drinks the water I give him will never thirst. Indeed, the water I give him will become in him a spring of water welling up to eternal life" (John 4:13-14).

Jesus said elsewhere, "I have come that they may have life, and have it to the full" (John 10:10). What Jesus is saying in these verses is that when we know him, and when we trust and obey him, we will be satisfied in him and we will not look elsewhere. When we are beholding the glory of God we will see the foolishness of worshipping people, places, and things. The reason we fall into the worship of the creation is that we, in our pride and idolatry, exchange the truth of God for a lie.

I used to have a beautiful bright ruby red 1992 Harley Davidson Low Rider motorcycle. This bike had several additional chrome accessories on it. Some of these pieces said, "Live to Ride, Ride to Live." I can remember sometime after becoming a Christian that this bothered me, so I put the original chrome pieces back onto the bike. This experience reminded me that before I became a Christian, I had, in my sinful pride, exchanged the truth of God for a lie and tried to

---

[8] John Piper, *Let the Nations be Glad* (Grand Rapids, MI: Baker Academic, 2003), 31.

find satisfaction in people, places, and things. But after being saved, I understood and was convinced that life was about living for the glory of God. I had come to understand what Paul meant when he wrote, "For to me, to live is Christ and to die is gain" (Philippians 1:21). To live for any other reason was not to live for the very purpose I was created for, and I did not want to give the impression that life was to be lived for any other reason. I still rode my Harley and enjoyed it, but I wasn't "living to ride." I had become overwhelmed by the love of God in Christ, and it was his love for me that was now motivating me to live for his glory.

The Bible tells us over and over that it is God's love that compels us to live for him. This simply means that as we are focused on God's love we will want to love him and love others. So, in light of this we obviously need to be convinced of his love.

Romans 12:1-2 says, "Therefore, I urge you, brothers, in view of God's mercy, to offer your bodies as living sacrifices, holy and pleasing to God—this is your spiritual act of worship. Do not conform any longer to the pattern of this world, but be transformed by the renewing of your mind. Then you will be able to test and approve what God's will is—his good, pleasing, and perfect will."

It is in view of God's mercy that we desire to submit to him. It is easy to get excited about God's love when we see the depths of our depravity, and yet understand that God sees us as perfect in Christ. "But in the gospel we discover that we are far more wicked than we ever dared believe, yet more loved than we ever dared hope."[9]

What a gospel! What a plan of redemption! Can you think of anything more amazing than the second person of the Trinity, God the Son, coming to earth, taking on human flesh,

---

[9] Keller, 64.

being born of a virgin, living a perfect life, voluntarily dying on a cross, being raised from the dead, ascending back to heaven, and promising to return? Why did God plan redemption in this way? He did this for his own glory. God receives true worship in response to the perfect love he has lavished on the sinful, wicked, and rebellious people he has called to salvation. Jesus lived the perfect life that God's holiness demands. He paid the full payment for our sins by dying on the cross as our substitute. He was raised from the dead to give us life, and he credits his perfect righteousness to our account.

Yet in spite of all he has done for us, we often are not convinced of his love and therefore do not live for his glory. We often look to the creation instead of the Creator. We need to be continually reminded that we are in the midst of real spiritual warfare (Ephesians 6:12). We are surrounded by a world system that rejects the truth of God (Ephesians 2:2; 1 John 2:15-17). In addition to all of this, we face an ongoing internal struggle in the depths of our being because of indwelling sin (Romans 7:14-25; Galatians 5:16-17). If only we were constantly convinced! If only we would take every thought captive and make it obedient to Christ (2 Corinthians 10:5).

The good news is that we will be constantly convinced of God's love in heaven. We will never fall into worshipping the creation in our resurrected bodies. But until glory we will continue to face this struggle. The apostle Paul knew this struggle. He said, "So I find this law at work: When I want to do good, evil is right there with me" (Romans 7:21). He goes on to say, "What a wretched man I am! Who will rescue me from this body of death? Thanks be to God—through Jesus Christ our Lord!" (Romans 7:24-25).

The apostle Paul understood this struggle, and he knew that the truth will set us free so that we can live for God's glory. That is why he wrote with full confidence, under the inspiration of the Holy Spirit in Romans chapter eight, "I am convinced." Let's look at these beautiful verses that God in his love has preserved for us in the book of Romans. I am going to break them down, verse-by-verse, so we can be convinced of them and then apply them to our life that we might live for God's glory.

> And we know that in all things God works for the good of those who love him, who have been called according to his purpose (Romans 8:28).

What a promise we have here. Paul says, "And we know." Paul is writing with deep conviction. He knows from Scripture that God cannot lie and that he never changes. Paul also knows this is true from his relationship with God through Christ. God always remains faithful to his word. What a firm foundation we have on which to stand. Paul is convinced of this promise for those whom God has called to salvation. What stability! What security! And this promise is for all things. Not just some things. Not just the good things. But *all* things; even those things we consider to be bad.

It is easy to praise God when things are going well. It is easy to be convinced that God loves us when things are going smoothly. But how about when things are not going so well? Do we glorify God in our thoughts, words, and actions then? How convinced are we in the trials and temptations of life?

It is during these times that we must look at everything in life in light of the cross. Knowing that we deserve nothing but eternal hell, yet also knowing that God loves us perfectly in Christ, puts everything into perspective. Is this always easy? No. Is it always true? Yes.

God worked for the good of those in Christ on the cross, and he will work for the good of those in Christ in all things. When we look seriously at the cross of Christ, it becomes difficult to doubt God's love.

Notice that verse 28 does not say that all things are good. It says that God works for the good in all things. Once again, we must look at the cross. Was it good for Jesus, the Holy One of God, to take upon himself the sin of the world? Was it good for him to cry out from the cross, "My God, my God, why have you forsaken me?" (Matthew 26:46). He had never felt separation from the Father before this. Was it good for him to suffer the horrendous flogging and crucifixion with the unthinkable pain that came with them? This doesn't sound very good to me. No amount of pain sounds good to me whether it be physical, emotional, or spiritual. I cannot imagine what it was like for the Holy One of God to go through this. Thanks be to Jesus!

The cross of Jesus Christ was, from a merely human perspective, the greatest tragedy in the history of the world. The completely innocent Son of God was brutally punished as a criminal. And yet from God's point of view and to those who are in Christ, it is the most beautiful act of love in the history of the world. Jesus voluntarily laid down his life for his sheep. He suffered and died for those who would believe.

God takes the worst event in the history of the world and makes it the greatest. Jesus' death on the cross provided full payment for the sins of those who believe in him, and his resurrection from the dead gives life and his own perfect righteousness to those who believe in him. The cross motivates us to live for God's glory.

Everything that happens in life is according to God's purpose (Ephesians 1:11). Notice I said *everything*. God is sovereign. God knows what will happen in the future because he has ordained it. God is holy. God is just. God is love. God is good. He can make death the way to life as he did with Jesus. He can take a curse and turn it into a blessing. He can take evil and work it for good. God works all things for the good of those who love him, who have been called according to his purpose (Romans 8:28). We can be convinced of God's love in all things.

Notice that the promise of Romans 8:28 is conditional. It says that God works all things for the good of those *who love him*. Do you love him? The Bible says, "We love because God first loved us" (1 John 4:19). It is impossible to truly love God unless we have first received his love for us. Once again, we cannot understand this unless we see who we are (depraved and wretched) and who God is (holy). God chooses to love those in Christ. There is no reason for him to love us. We can offer him nothing. He just chooses to lavish his love on us. That is what makes his love so amazing. And that is why we can be convinced!

> And we know that in all things God works for the good of those who love him, who have been called according to his purpose. For those God foreknew he also predestined to be conformed to the likeness of his Son, that he might be the firstborn among many brothers. And those he predestined, he also called; those he called, he also justified; those he justified, he also glorified (Romans 8:28-30).

We must read verse 28 in connection with verse 29, which says, "For those God foreknew he also predestined to be conformed to the likeness of his Son, that he might be the firstborn among many brothers." This verse gives us at least part of the answer as to why things happen. It gives us a glimpse into part of God's plan.

We have no problem with the good things that come our way in life. But we usually have a problem with the things we see as bad. The Bible teaches that God is sovereign over all things. So everything that happens is ultimately part of his plan. Verse 29 tells us why—or at least part of the reason—these things happen. It is through these very things that the sovereign God transforms us to the likeness of Christ. God is using everything that happens to us, good and bad, for our ultimate good, and most importantly, for his glory. This includes all the trials we face in life. This even includes the sins others commit against us.

We have the account in 2 Samuel 16:5-14 of a man named Shimei who was cursing and throwing stones at King David and David's men. David could have responded in fear, anger, pride, and idolatry and had the man killed. Yet David was convinced of God's love for him. How did David respond? He responded in humility and worship. He said, "It may be that the Lord will see my distress and repay me with good for the cursing I am receiving today" (2 Samuel 16:12).

David was, at this moment anyway, convinced of God's love for him. God worked this situation out for the good of David. David focused on God's sovereignty and goodness and therefore trusted that God would work this to good rather than focusing on what Shimei was doing to him. God used this incident in the sanctification process for David. God also used the example of David in this confrontation to teach the others who were with him to live for God's glory, and not their own. David taught them not to fear man, but to fear God. He taught them not to gossip and slander others even when others sin against them. Because David was controlled in this trial by the love of God, he did not fear rejection from man. That is why

David did not respond with anger. God's love for David is what compelled David to trust and obey. In this circumstance, as he was convinced of God's love, he was living for God's glory and not his own.

How can we apply this to our lives? God wants to use all the things in our lives, as he did with David's, to conform us to the image of Christ. The next time someone does something to you and your feelings get hurt, think of how God may be using that event to cleanse you from the idol of the fear of man, and instead, directing you to fear him and rest in his perfect love for you in Christ. He wants us to be convinced of his love. God ordains conflict for his glory so that we might become convinced and become more like Jesus.

If you are in Christ, God chose you by an eternal decision on his part. He predestined that you would become his for his glory. Doesn't that convince you of his love? If not, believe it, because he has said it, and he cannot lie. Then you will feel it. The Bible teaches us that our emotions follow our thinking (Philippians 4:4-9).

If you are in Christ, God chose you to be called to salvation. He also called you to become conformed to the likeness of Christ through all things, and you have the promise that one day you will receive a perfect resurrected body like Christ's. All of this is as good as done in the mind of God. We see this in Romans 8:30 from the use of the past tense of the verbs. We can count it as a sure and secure thing that will happen. We can be convinced. God cannot lie and he does not change.

> And those he predestined, he also called; those he called, he also justified; those he justified, he also glorified (Romans 8:30).

This verse tells us that God, in eternity past, predestined to salvation those he will call. And those he will call will be justified. And those called and justified will be glorified. What security there is in the eternal decisions of God! He is not like man, who lies and changes his mind from one moment to the next.

There is no hope or satisfaction in the worship of people, places, or things. There is hope and satisfaction in the worship of God alone. If you have been called into Christ, God made this decision from eternity past and it has always been as good as done. You would not be able to change it even if you wanted to. Needless to say, no one who has truly been called would ever want to. Those who truly come to Christ do so willingly (John 6:37, 45).

Jesus said, "I give them eternal life, and they shall never perish; no one can snatch them out of my hand" (John 10:28). Guess what—this includes the devil. Is he stronger than God? Does his decision overpower the eternal decision of God? If so, you have a very weak god who is not in control of this universe.

We can rest in the perfect love of a God who chose us before the foundation of the world in Christ. God's promises always come with guarantees that never wear out. We can and we must be convinced! It is God's love that compels us to trust and obey him (2 Corinthians 5:14-15). When we trust and obey, God gets the glory and we experience life to the full. Live for God's glory. To live for anything or anyone else is to reject the very purpose for which God predestined you, called you, justified you, and will glorify you. "For to me, to live is Christ and to die is gain" (Philippians 1:21).

Questions and Prayer

1. For whom or for what are you living? If you are not living for God's glory, do you think that whatever you are living for will completely satisfy you? What did the woman at the well find out in John 4:10-18?

2. What would you say are biblical motives for living for God's glory? What are unbiblical motives for living for God's glory? Pray that God will help you see your motives.

3. What situations are you experiencing right now that you need to trust God to work for good? Pray about these and believe God's promise to you in Christ. When you struggle, remember the cross.

4. What lessons can you learn and apply to your life from how David responded with humility and worship, instead of pride and idolatry, in 2 Samuel 16:5-14? Ask God to help you.

Chapter 6

God Is for You!

"What then shall we say in response to all of this? If God is for us, who can be against us?" (Romans 8:31).

What confident trust in God this verse gives to those in Christ. It is easy to memorize the phrase, "God is for us." The problem is that it is not so easy for us to be convinced. This problem has nothing to do with God. He cannot lie and he never changes. God is for us whether we believe it or not. That is where the problem lies. We choose not to believe it. In pride and idolatry we once again exchange the truth of God for a lie.

We can memorize the whole Bible and yet not believe it, and therefore it will have no effect on our lives. We can even say we believe it and yet there will be no effect on our lives. We must trust and obey. We must not be merely hearers of the word, but also doers of the word (James 1:22).

I strongly recommend that you memorize the truth, "If God is for us, who can be against us?" (Romans 8:31). I also recommend that you not only memorize it, but become convinced of its truth, and then act on it. This simple verse will set you free from many thoughts, words, and actions that are against God's will and are destructive.

If you are convinced that God is for you, then you will trust and obey him in every situation in life. Just a few examples of this include being able to receive correction in humility instead of anger, remaining committed to your marriage when things are difficult, and being full of praise and thanksgiving instead of complaining and discontentment.

Let me ask you a question: Do you know anyone greater than God? Let's think about this for a moment. God is all-powerful, all-knowing, and everywhere present. He can never lie and he does not change. This God has said that in all things he works for the good of those who love him and are called according to his purpose (Romans 8:28). He is presently conforming us to the image of Christ (Romans 8:29). He has chosen us before the creation of the world (Ephesians 1:4). He has called us, he has justified us, and he will glorify us (Romans 8:30). What, then, shall we say in response to all of this (Romans 8:31)? We can say with confidence that if God is for us, nothing can be against us. The "if" here means "because." This is not a question of maybe or doubt. This is a promise that if you are in Christ, God is for you. Even if no one else is for you, guess what—God is! And his opinion is by far the most important. He is the Creator. All others are the creation. His opinion does not change; others' opinions are constantly changing.

Let me ask you another question: What can be against you? God is all-powerful. He is all-knowing. He is everywhere present. He is holy. He is perfect love. He can never lie and he does not change. The promise that God is for you will set you free not only when people are against you, but also when the circumstances of life seem to be against you. Whatever God has planned to come your way is going to be used to conform you to the image of Christ. Everything God does has a redemptive purpose behind it. You will trust and obey God when you are convinced of his love for you in Christ. We will see this truth more deeply in the upcoming verses of Romans eight.

Just stop for a moment and consider the truth that if you are in Christ, God is for you. This isn't true just some of the time. This is true all of the time. This is true even when you do not "feel" God: when you think he is absent, when you think he has forgotten about you, or when you think you have totally blown it. I am compelled to remind you who profess to be in Christ that we do not discern what is true by our feelings. We discern what is true by the objective word of God. God has said it and that is final. If you are in Christ, he is for you, so who can be against you? Believe it. Be convinced!

Why should you be convinced? Because God has said so in his written word and he has shown you by sending the Living Word, Jesus.

> What then shall we say in response to this? If God is for us, who can be against us? He who did not spare his own Son, but gave him up for us all—how will he not also, along with him, graciously give us all things? (Romans 8:31-32).

Are we to think that the God of the universe, who did not spare even his own Son, would give him up to suffer and die for us, and then choose not to be for us? That he would somehow be against us? Very bad theology, is it not? Let us not forget what the Bible says about our goodness. We do not have any apart from Christ. He died for us while we were still sinners (Romans 5:8). Is he now going to reject us after we have become children of God in Christ? No way! God has never failed in his redemptive work and he never will.

I do not believe for one second that God wasted his Son's time living on earth, dying on a cross, and being raised from the dead. Would God send his one and only Son to suffer and die for those who would believe, and then turn his back on them? Would Jesus reject the very ones he died for?

If you are in Christ, God has, once and for all time, proven his love for you by not sparing his one and only Son that he gave up for you. How can we doubt that God is for us in light of the cross? Yet we do just that on a regular basis. We often doubt just like the disciples who walked with Christ did. For example, do you remember when Jesus, the Lamb of God who came to take away the sins of the world (John 1:29), tells his disciples that he is going to suffer, die, and be raised from the dead (Mark 8:31)? He has come into the world to seek and save what was lost (Luke 19:10). Yet the disciples, shortly after hearing that Jesus would suffer and die, argue about which of them will be the greatest in the kingdom. Talk about the two-sided coin of pride/idolatry! The only one who can love perfectly is right there with them, about to show his love on the cross. This is God, the Creator, and yet the disciples start exchanging the truth of God for a lie and worship and serve created things (Romans 1:25). They are seeking the love and acceptance of people. They are worshipping places of status and honor because they are not resting in God's love. Likewise, we often fail to be convinced, and living on this side of the death and resurrection, we have a greater understanding of the person and work of Jesus than they did. May we just look at the cross and be convinced!

If you are convinced that God is for you even when others are not, you will be loving in your thoughts, words, and actions. You can rest in God's love. You can remain humble. For this to become a reality, you must be controlled by the Holy Spirit. You must depend upon God (John 15:5). You must offer yourself as a living sacrifice by faith (Romans 12:1-2). To walk in the Spirit is to be controlled by the love of God. It is to be convinced of the width, length, height, and depth of the love of Christ (Ephesians 3:16-19). If you are controlled by, consumed with, and focused on God's love, his love will naturally flow out of you to others. We love because God first loved us (1 John 4:19). If in your fear of man, you are worshipping the love of others, love will not flow out of you.

Some caution is necessary at this point to help prevent any misunderstandings of the importance of knowing that God is for you. This verse has been abused and taken out of context many times and in many different ways. For example, I have heard this verse quoted by professional athletes at the end of a game as the reason that they or their team won. Is their application of this verse correct? Is it true that they won the game because God is for them? Does this mean that God is not for the Christians on the losing team? Obviously this is not a good use of this verse. In reality, God ordained which team would win as part of his sovereign plan for his purposes. Other people misquote this verse when they are confronted with sin and respond in pride by saying something along the lines of, "I do not care what you say. God is for me." Really? Can you quote this verse to avoid dealing with your sin? Is God for our sin? Obviously God is never for our sin. Others use this verse to try and make them feel good about themselves or to make themselves feel special. Is that really why God gave us this verse? Does God want us to focus on how special we are? In all three of these examples the focus is on the person rather than God. This leads to a man-centered theology rather than a God-centered theology.

Romans 8:31 is in the context of what God has done in saving his people through Jesus Christ. The verses before and after verse 31 are very clearly focused on God's plan in saving us. The focus is on what God has done in our salvation and what God is doing in our sanctification. The point of verse 31 is that no one can bring a charge of eternal condemnation and a final verdict of guilty on those in Christ because if we are in Christ there is no condemnation awaiting us (Romans 8:1). If we are in Christ God has saved us. If we are in Christ he has taken our sins away and he has credited his righteousness to us. Therefore we stand not guilty in his sight both now and forever. God is for us according to his perfect will. He is eternally for us because of what Christ has done. And he is for us in the here and now (according to his purpose for his glory) in his working all things to good to make us more like Christ (Romans 8:28-29). He is also for us in that we can never be separated from his love regardless of what trials we will face (Romans 8:32-39).

So, we can be convinced that no matter what comes our way in life, God is for us according to his will and his purpose is to make us more like Christ. When we are convinced that God is for us in this way we will respond in humility and worship rather than pride and idolatry.

Let us not exchange the truth of God for a lie and worship and serve created things (Romans 1:25). Let us be convinced that if God is for us, no one or no thing can ever possibly be against us (Romans 8:31).

> Who will bring any charge against those whom God has chosen? It is God who justifies. Who is he that condemns? Christ Jesus, who died—more than that, who was raised to life—is at the right hand of God and is also interceding for us (Romans 8:33-34).

Who will bring a charge against us? No one can. Those who are in Christ are seen in God's sight as perfect. How is it possible for God to see sinful wretched people such as us as perfect? That is the reason Jesus came to earth. He lived a perfect life for us. Jesus' perfect life is credited to the account of those who repent of their sins, who trust his death on the cross as full payment for those sins, and who look to his resurrection as their only hope of eternal life. God's standard to enter heaven is perfection. He is holy. That perfection must be given to us from the perfect One.

In Hebrews we read, "It is impossible for the blood of bulls and goats to take away sins. Therefore, when Christ came into the world, he said: 'Sacrifice and offering you did not desire, but a body you prepared for me'" (Hebrews 10:4-5). An animal is not a moral creature. Animals are not made in God's image. There was a need for a perfect human to die as a substitute for our sins.

In the Old Testament, the sacrifices had to be without physical blemish or defect. This was a picture of the final sacrifice who would come, the one who would be without blemish or defect.

> For you know that it was not with perishable things such as silver or gold that you were redeemed from the empty way of life handed down to you from your forefathers, but with the precious blood of Christ, a lamb without blemish or defect. He was chosen before the foundation of the world, but was revealed in these last times for your sake (1 Peter 1:18-20).

Here we are told that Jesus, the Lamb of God who takes away the sins of the world, was without blemish or defect. He never sinned. He lived a perfect life in thought, word, and deed. The only way for sinful humanity to be redeemed was through a perfect human life sacrificed as a substitute for our sins. His perfect life qualified him to die for our sins.

> But now he has reconciled you by Christ's physical body through his death to present you holy in his sight, without blemish and free from accusation (Colossians 1:22).

What a plan of redemption! The Bible plainly tells us that Jesus lived a perfect life (2 Corinthians 5:21). This perfect life qualified him to die as our substitute on the cross. Then he was raised from the dead. We are told that those who are in Christ are holy in his sight and their sins have been taken away. What more can we ask for? What more can we want? God loves us perfectly in Christ. His perfect love motivates us to live for him.

It is God who justifies. He has taken our sins away in Christ and he has given us his righteousness in Christ. Who can bring a charge on those whom God says are righteous? How foolish it would be to try to do so. God is the perfect and just judge. His verdict stands.

God has chosen those in Christ and he has pronounced that they are justified. There can be no appeal. His decision was set before the foundation of the world. Who is going to change that? God has called those in Christ justified. He sees us as perfect. In light of these facts, does it really matter what others think of us unless we are outside of God's will? God has chosen to love us perfectly and he knows all of those wicked thoughts, words, and actions that nobody else knows about. Yet he still loves us in Christ. Do you want anyone else to know everything you have thought, said, and done? Of course not! So why do we worship their love and acceptance? Why do we fear man? God is the only one who will never reject us. Let's fear him and rest in his love.

Therefore, there is now no condemnation for those who are in Christ Jesus (Romans 8:1).

Even if the whole world would condemn us, if we are in Christ, God never will. We are told that Jesus is always interceding for us to the Father (Hebrews 7:25). No matter who brings an accusation against us, Jesus will always cover it. I am writing here about our position in Christ. I am writing about how God views us in Christ as his children. This does not mean that God will never discipline us because of the sins we commit. God is the most loving Father. God is perfect love, and therefore God disciplines his children.

Because the Lord disciplines those he loves, and he punishes everyone he accepts as a son (Hebrews 12:6).

Keep in mind that God still hates sin and he always will. Yet he sees those who are in Christ as perfect, and in his perfect love he will discipline them when needed. This, too, is God working for the good of those who love him (Romans 8:28). Everything is good with God.

We can be convinced that God loves us in Christ, and we can be convinced that if God is for us nothing and no one can be against us (Romans 8:31, 38-39). In the next chapter we will see how we can remain convinced of these promises in the trials of life.

Questions and Prayer

1. Whom do you see as being against you right now? What circumstances do you see as being against you right now? How will knowing that God is for you enable you to glorify God in these relationships and situations?

2. How can focusing on the cross help you when it seems that people and circumstances are against you? Why does the cross prove that God is always for you?

3. How is it possible for God to see sinful wretched people like us as perfect?

4. Memorize Romans 8:31 and pray that you will be convinced that God is for you. Trust God's Word rather than your feelings.

Chapter 7

Being Convinced in Trials

"Who shall separate us from the love of Christ? Shall trouble or hardship or persecution or famine or nakedness or danger or sword? As it is written: 'For your sake we face death all day long; we are considered as sheep to be slaughtered'" (Romans 8:35-36).

If we are in Christ we have already determined from Scripture that nothing can separate us from the love of Christ. This is objective truth. This can never change. What does change is our subjective feelings. When our minds are not convinced of the perfect love we have in Christ, we then "feel" separate from his love, even though, in fact, we are not. We must "take captive every thought to make it obedient to Christ" (2 Corinthians 10:5). Taking every thought captive means that we replace unbiblical thinking with biblical thinking. The truth will set us free (John 8:32).

As Christians, we do not, or at least we should not, base reality on our feelings or on what we think is true. The word of God is true; and when we trust and obey what God has said, our feelings will fall in line with what is true. Truth is determined by what God says, not by what we think or feel.

It is often difficult for us to focus on God's truth when we face the trials of life. Let's be honest. It is difficult because we focus on our circumstances rather than on the God who is above, in control of, and has even ordained our circumstances. Our pride and unbelief is often seen in the midst of our trials. Often, in the midst of the trials of life, we do not believe that God is working for the good. We do not trust that God is good and loving. Why? We are not convinced of the truth that nothing can separate us from the love of God in Christ Jesus (Romans 8:39). We are focused on our subjective thoughts and feelings rather than on God's truth. Often, in our pride we think we can do something to control our circumstances, and in our idolatry we worship ourselves and/or other false gods.

We can find help in our trials through Philippians 4:6-7, which says, "Do not be anxious about anything, but in everything, by prayer and petition, with thanksgiving, present your requests to God. And the peace of God, which transcends all understanding, will guard your hearts and minds in Christ Jesus."

The key to experiencing the peace of God is praying with thanksgiving. Praying with thanksgiving means we pray like we know that nothing can separate us from the love of Christ. We pray with thanksgiving when we pray with the knowledge and trust that God is in control and that he has our best interest in mind, which is to conform us to the likeness of Christ (Romans 8:28-29). The key is that we must really believe and we must really be convinced of God's promises. When we are convinced we experience the supernatural peace of God. We can rejoice in the Lord always (Philippians 4:4). When we are not convinced we experience fear that can lead to impatience, anger, etc. and we often try to "fix" things outside of

God's moral will. When this happens we have fallen into idolatry again as we attempt to play God in trying to control things.

If you are going through a very difficult time right now, my heart goes out to you. I do not say what I am about to say lightly or with indifference to your circumstances. But I am compelled to say it; therefore, I do so with gentleness and respect but with boldness as well because it is true, and it has set me free on many occasions. If you are in Christ you know that what I am about to say is true. If you are not in Christ you will likely despise it. The truth always divides. The humble love it and the proud hate it. But here it goes: The reality of life is that the only thing we deserve is eternal conscious torment in hell, so whatever we have to go through this side of eternity, as difficult as it may be, is not as bad as what we deserve. This truth knocks everything down. Hell puts everything into perspective.

Let us never forget that the sinless Son of God suffered the wrath of God on the cross for the sins of those who would receive him. We will never suffer that much and we are sinful. It is God's eternal love that has rescued those in Christ from eternal conscious torment in hell through Jesus, who voluntarily, out of love, took the wrath we deserve.

When we are suffering we must look to the cross. There, and there alone, will we find abundant mercy, grace, love, peace, and even joy. Nothing can separate us from the love of Christ.

Shall Trouble Separate Us From the Love of Christ?

> God is our refuge and strength, an ever-present help in trouble (Psalm 46:1).

> I have told you these things, so that in me you may have peace. In this world you will have trouble. But take heart! I have overcome the world. (John 16:33)

> Therefore we do not lose heart. Though outwardly we are wasting away, yet inwardly we are being renewed day by day. For our light and momentary troubles are achieving for us an eternal glory that far outweighs them all. So we fix our eyes not on what is seen, but on what is unseen. For what is seen is temporary, but what is unseen is eternal (2 Corinthians 4:16-18).

God is always there for us if we are in Christ. He has promised never to leave us nor forsake us (Hebrews 13:5). Psalm 46 teaches us that God alone is to be our refuge and strength. We are not to seek refuge in the worship of people, places, and things. God has ordained certain means such as Christian fellowship to help us in times of trouble and we should use them, but they are not to replace God as our all-sufficient refuge and strength. God has promised us that we will face trouble in this troubled world. He has also promised us that he has overcome the world. We can have peace when we trust his unfailing love in the midst of our trouble.

When we fix our eyes on God's truth instead of our circumstances, we will not lose heart. We are to live by faith and not by sight (2 Corinthians 5:7). Trouble cannot separate us from the love of Christ. Be convinced!

Shall Hardship Separate Us From the Love of Christ?

> That is why, for Christ's sake, I delight in weaknesses, in insults, in hardships, in persecutions, in

difficulties. For when I am weak, then I am strong (2 Corinthians 12:10).

Endure hardship as discipline; God is treating you as sons. For what son is not disciplined by his father? ... Our fathers disciplined us for a little while as they thought best; but God disciplines us for our good that we may share in his holiness. No discipline seems pleasant at the time, but painful. Later on, however, it produces a harvest of righteousness and peace for those who have been trained by it (Hebrews 12:7, 10-11).

You have persevered and have endured hardships for my name, and have not grown weary (Revelation 2:3).

Paul delighted in hardship because it drove him to the love of Christ. By resting in the love of Christ, we, too, can endure hardship. Hardship can be a blessing as we grow in trusting God's love for us. God's discipline toward us always comes from his love for us, and his purpose is to conform us to the image of Christ. The only way we can persevere and endure hardship for Jesus' name and glory is to be controlled by the love of God in Christ Jesus. If we are controlled by our hardships instead of by the love of God, we will neither persevere nor endure them for his glory. Hardships cannot separate us from the love of Christ. Be convinced!

Shall Persecution Separate Us From the Love of Christ?

When they heard this, they were furious and gnashed their teeth at him. But Stephen, full of the

Holy Spirit, looked up to heaven and saw the glory of God, and Jesus standing at the right hand of God. "Look," he said, "I see heaven open and the Son of Man standing at the right hand of God." At this they covered their ears and, yelling at the top of their voices, they all rushed at him, dragged him out of the city and began to stone him. Meanwhile, the witnesses laid their clothes at the feet of a young man named Saul. While they were stoning him, Stephen prayed, "Lord Jesus, receive my spirit." Then he fell on his knees and cried out, "Lord, do not hold this sin against them." When he had said this, he fell asleep (Acts 7:54-60).

From Stephen's experience we see that persecution does not separate us from the love of Christ. In fact, there may be no other time when we experience God's love more gloriously. Stephen was completely controlled by the love of God. He saw the one who suffered and died for him in the midst of his own suffering. He was full of the Holy Spirit, which means he was full of God's love. How else could he have said, "Lord, do not hold this sin against them" (Acts 7:60)? Persecution cannot separate us from the love of Christ. Be convinced!

Shall Famine Separate Us From the Love of Christ?

In Genesis chapters 37-50 we have all the proof we need that famine cannot separate us from the love of Christ. In this account, Joseph, the son of Jacob, was sold into slavery by his jealous and murderous brothers. Afterward he was taken to Egypt, where, through a series of events, he became second in command only to the Pharaoh himself. During this time there was a famine in Egypt and in Canaan, Joseph's homeland. So

Joseph's brothers left Canaan and went to Egypt to buy grain. There was food in Egypt because God had given Joseph the wisdom to store grain during the years before the famine. Eventually Jacob and all his sons were spared from famine as they came to get food in Egypt and even ended up moving there to live. It was God, in his gracious and loving plan, who sustained his people during the famine.

In Matthew 6 we are told that if God feeds the birds of the air, will he not feed us (Matthew 6:26)? We are also told that if we first seek God's kingdom and his righteousness, we will be given all that we need (Matthew 6:33). Famine cannot separate us from the love of Christ. Be convinced!

Shall Nakedness Separate Us From the Love of Christ?

> And why do you worry about clothes? See how the lilies of the field grow. They do not labor or spin. Yet I tell you that not even Solomon in all his splendor was dressed like one of these. If that is how God clothes the grass of the field, which is here today and tomorrow is thrown into the fire, will he not much more clothe you, O you of little faith? (Matthew 6:28-30).

Once again we have promises from a loving Father who will care for us. He knows what we need. He will clothe us. Nakedness cannot separate us from the love of Christ. Let us never forget the most gracious act of God by which he has clothed our spiritual nakedness with the righteousness of Christ. We see this from the beginning when God clothed Adam and Eve with animal skins after the fall into sin (Genesis 3:21). This is a picture of the final sacrifice: Jesus' being sacrificed for our sins so that we could be clothed in his perfection. Be convinced!

Shall Danger Separate Us From the Love of Christ?

> I have been constantly on the move. I have been in danger from rivers, in danger from bandits, in danger from my own countrymen, in danger from Gentiles; in danger in the city, in danger in the country, in danger at sea; and in danger from false brothers (2 Corinthians 11:26).

Paul experienced just about every kind of danger we can think of, yet he writes to us that nothing can separate us from the love of Christ. God has ordained any danger that we will face in life for his purposes. Just think of the account of the disciples in the boat when the storm came upon them (Matthew 14:22-34). Jesus told them to get into the boat. They got into the boat and he came to their rescue. All of this happened to reveal his glory to them. Everything that happens in our lives is meant to reveal God's glory to us. Danger cannot separate us from the love of Christ. In fact, it should cause us to depend on his love even more. Be convinced!

Shall the Sword Separate Us From the Love of Christ?

> Not even death can separate us from the love of Christ. As a matter of fact, for those of us in Christ, it is death that brings us to be in the physical presence of Christ and his love. In heaven there will never be a time when we will not be totally convinced of the love of God that is in Christ Jesus. We have a twelve-year-old daughter named Anna and a nine-year-old daughter named Leah. I have heard them say, "I cannot wait

to be with Jesus." That should be the cry of all those who are in Christ. Paul said, "For to me, to live is Christ and to die is gain" (Philippians 1:21). The sword cannot separate us from the love of Christ. Be convinced!

Suffering Does Not Separate Us From the Love of Christ!

> Who shall separate us from the love of Christ? Shall trouble or hardship or persecution or famine or nakedness or danger or sword? As it is written: 'For your sake we face death all day long; we are considered as sheep to be slaughtered' (Romans 8:35-36).

I hope and pray that you have not been deceived by the so-called "prosperity gospel" that is so prevalent in our culture today. It is no gospel at all. It was not the gospel of Jesus or any of the apostles. It was not the gospel of the early church, and it is not the gospel of the church today. The prosperity gospel is made up of nothing more than Satan's lies masquerading as truth. Please do not misunderstand me. When we obey God we will always prosper spiritually, but there is no biblical promise that we will always prosper in our health and our wealth.

In Romans 8:36 Paul quotes Psalm 44:22. Suffering has always been a part of life for God's people on this side of glory. Suffering is part of the road to glory. Through it we are refined as though through fire. Through it God tests us. Do we respond with faith or unbelief? Are we convinced that nothing can separate us from the love of God in Christ Jesus and that he is for us? Or do we fall prey to our circumstances? Everything in life is meant for God's glory. It is for God's glory that we face the sufferings and trials of life. We can be convinced in the midst of them. Be convinced!

Is God's Word a Priority in Your life?

> For everything that was written in the past was written to teach us, so that through endurance and the encouragement of the Scriptures we might have hope (Romans 15:4).

I cannot imagine life without knowing the love of God. For 28 years I lived without it. I worshipped the creation—people, places, and things—and I never found true love though I went many places, had many things, and knew many people. I am very grateful to God for choosing me to be in Christ. I am grateful for the Scriptures that tell me that nothing can separate me from the love of God in Christ Jesus. I am thankful for the many examples of faith in the Bible. For I am surrounded by a great cloud of witnesses who knew God's love and expressed this love through faith (Hebrews 12:1). We should never take the awesome privilege of having God's word for granted.

We must take God's word seriously. The Bible is God's love letter written to those in Christ. I must ask you what priority you place on the word of God. If you do not spend time with God in his word you will never become truly convinced of God's love, and you will not experience his love radically changing your everyday life. Spend time with God in his word on a daily basis, be convinced by what it says, and apply it to your life.

Questions and Prayer

1. Pray that God will help you focus on his character and his promises in the midst of the trials you are facing.

2. How can knowing that God is above, in control of, and has even ordained all of your circumstances give you peace in the midst of trials?

3. Life can be very difficult and we do not always think clearly. Yet how can reflecting on the fact that the only thing you deserve is eternal conscious torment in Hell give you a new perspective in your trials, especially in light of the mercy and grace you have been given in Christ?

4. Do you really believe that nothing can separate you from God's love? Why or why not?

5. Make it a priority to spend time each day with God in his word and in prayer. Then trust and obey him.

Chapter 8

For I Am Convinced!

"No, in all these things we are more than conquerors through him who loved us. *For I am convinced* that neither death nor life, neither angels nor demons, neither the present nor the future, nor any powers, neither height nor depth, nor anything else in all creation, will be able to separate us from the love of God that is in Christ Jesus our Lord" (Romans 8:37-39, emphasis mine).

The question we dealt with in the last chapter is, "Who shall separate us from the love of Christ? Shall trouble or hardship or persecution or famine or nakedness or danger or sword?" (Romans 8:35). In verse 37 Paul tells us that the answer is a resounding "nothing" and "no one." He goes on to tell us that not only can nothing or no one separate us from the love of God in Christ Jesus, but we are more than conquerors through him who loved us (Romans 8:37).

Many people would claim that they have conquered something in life. Yet many times after the excitement of the conquest fades away they do not remain content. Surely this has been the case throughout the history of the world as powerful nations, rulers, and tyrants have defeated different groups of people in their greed and idolatrous worship of power and wealth. If you are a sports fan you most likely have known of professional athletes who have set several records or won the biggest games or events in their sport, yet after their "victory" they do not remain satisfied for long. Why do they not remain satisfied? They do not remain satisfied because the things of this life, the temporal things, can never satisfy the human heart. Jesus said, "Everyone who drinks this water will be thirsty again, but whoever drinks the water I give him will never thirst. Indeed, the water I give him will become in him a spring of water welling up to eternal life" (John 4:13-14).

Likewise, many people have endured many things. They have "made it through." They've pulled themselves up and we hear them say things such as, "Well, under the circumstances I am doing as well as can be expected."

Please do not get me wrong here. Life can be terribly difficult. I thank God for his common grace that gets people through painful circumstances. Yet Paul is telling us that we do not have to just "get through" things as Christians. We do not have to just endure things and smile on the outside while being miserable on the inside. We do not have to live under our circumstances. We can be filled with God's unfailing love no matter how horrible our circumstances are. We truly can be more than conquerors through Christ.

The only thing that makes this possible is his love for us. As Paul said, "No, in all these things we are more than conquerors through him who *loved* us" (Romans 8:37, emphasis mine). When we are focused on the cross, seeing what Christ went through for us, and how he was more than a conqueror over sin and death, and when we are filled with his love in the power of the Holy Spirit, we, too, can be more than conquerors. This is why God says to us, "Rejoice in the Lord always. I will say it again: Rejoice!" (Philippians 4:4) and "Be joyful always; pray continually; give thanks in all circumstances, for this is God's will for you in Christ Jesus" (1 Thessalonians 5:16-18).

Being joyful always and giving thanks in all circumstances is being more than a conqueror. This kind of living is not just getting through our trials, but getting through them while remaining convinced that God is for us and loves us. This kind of living is like flying over the circumstances of life and looking down on them from God's perspective. No one can be more than a conqueror unless he is convinced of God's perfect love for him in Christ. This can happen only through him who loves us.

Being more than a conqueror is more than just making it through circumstances without getting fearful and angry. Being more than a conqueror is having peace and joy in the midst of any circumstance. Being more than a conqueror is more than not taking revenge or getting even; it is repaying evil with good, praying for those who mistreat us, and loving them in our hearts. Being more than a conqueror can take place only when God conquers our pride and idolatry and we are convinced of his love. When this happens we exchange our pride and idolatry for humility and worship.

I cannot answer for you, but I want to be more than a conqueror. I will not always live up to this, but I do want to grow in this area. To do this I know that I must be convinced that nothing can separate me from the love of God in Christ Jesus. I must take God at his word. It is easy for us to be convinced of things we can see, touch, taste, smell, and hear. We are motivated to eat because we are convinced that food will satisfy our hunger. We are motivated to drink because we are convinced that water will quench our thirst. We are motivated to sleep because we are convinced that sleep will refresh us.

When it comes to the things we cannot see, however, we will be motivated to trust and obey our Lord only when we are convinced that nothing can separate us from the love of God. This requires faith. "Faith is being sure of what we hope for and certain of what we do not see" (Hebrews 11:1). We are convinced only when we are living by faith. We could very easily substitute the word "convinced" for the words "sure" and "certain" in Hebrews 11:1. If you are sure and certain, then you are surely and certainly convinced.

> For I am *convinced* that neither death nor life, neither angels nor demons, neither the present nor the future, nor any powers, neither height nor depth, nor anything else in all creation, will be able to separate us from the love of God that is in Christ Jesus our Lord (Romans 8:38-39, emphasis mine).

Here it is! Here is one of the greatest keys, if not the greatest key, to maturity in Christ! Here is a specially marked door to humility and worship. Here, once again, is that often repeated biblical motivation for fearing God and thus trusting and obeying him. Paul says that he is *convinced*. Let me repeat that. Paul says that he is *convinced*. Why is Paul convinced? First, he is convinced on the basis of what God has said. God cannot lie. He does not break his promises and he always keeps his word. Second, Paul is convinced on the basis of who God is, which is revealed to us in Scripture. God is unchanging. Knowing that God is unchanging, we can have great hope and confidence in who this unchanging God is and what an unchanging God will do. God, who is loving, holy, and just, will always be loving, holy, and just. Last, Paul is convinced based on his personal experience with God's love in the midst of suffering. He had suffered just about everything possible, yet he remained convinced that nothing could separate him from the love of God in Christ Jesus. Let's look at some of the things Paul went through in life:

> I have worked much harder, been in prison more frequently, been flogged more severely, and been exposed to death again and again. Five times I received from the Jews the forty lashes minus one. Three times I was beaten with rods, once I was stoned, three times I was shipwrecked, I spent a night and a day in the open sea, I have been constantly on the move. I have been in danger from rivers, in danger from bandits, in danger from my own countrymen, in danger from Gentiles; in danger in the city, in danger in the country, in danger at sea; and in danger from false brothers. I have labored and toiled and have often gone without sleep; I have known hunger and thirst and have often gone without food; I have been cold and naked. Besides everything else, I face daily the pressure of my concern for all the churches. Who is weak, and I do not feel weak? Who is led into sin, and I do not inwardly burn? If I must boast, I will boast of the things that show my weakness. The God and Father of the Lord Jesus, who is to be praised forever, knows that I am not lying. In Damascus the governor under King Aretas had the city of the Damascenes guarded in order to arrest me. But I was lowered in a basket from a window in the wall and slipped through his hands (2 Corinthians 11:23-33).

Paul experienced some extremely serious trials. He was an apostle divinely chosen by the Lord. Paul wrote more of the inspired, infallible, and inerrant books of the New Testament than any other writer. He was an eyewitness to the risen Lord. Paul had the authority given to him by God to write to us so that we can be convinced that nothing can separate us from the love of God in Christ Jesus.

> For I am convinced that neither death nor life, neither angels nor demons, neither the present nor the future, nor any powers, neither height nor depth, nor anything else in all creation, will be able to separate us from the love of God that is in Christ Jesus our Lord (Romans 8:38-39).

Paul listed several things in verse 35, which we looked at in the last chapter, that cannot separate us from the love of Christ. Here in verses 38 and 39 he covers everything else — just in case, in our pride/idolatry, we try to find something else that can. Let's look at them more closely.

How could Paul say in Romans 8:38 that he was convinced that death could not separate us from the love of God in Christ Jesus?

> For to me, to live is Christ and to die is gain. If I am to go on living in the body, this will mean fruitful labor for me. Yet what shall I choose? I do not know! I am torn between the two; I desire to depart and be with Christ, which is better by far; but it is more necessary for you that I remain in the body (Philippians 1:21-24).

Paul knew that for a Christian, to die is gain. If we are in Christ we have eternal life. Paul desired to be with Christ. He said that it is better by far to die and be with Christ. That should be the cry of every Christian. We long for heaven. We long to be with Christ, we long to be out of this body that struggles with sin and all of its infirmities. I do not mean that we should despise life here on earth. Those in Christ should live a life of joy. Joy is lasting and comes from the Holy Spirit. Happiness is fleeting and temporal. Yet as much as we enjoy life here, we know it is even better to be with Christ. In the meantime, while we are on earth, we know that God still has work for us to do, and we should desire to glorify him in everything.

Paul says in this passage from the book of Philippians that "It is more necessary for you that I remain in the body." Paul is telling us that life here on earth is not about us. We are to love the Lord with our total being, and we are to love our neighbor as ourselves. It is necessary for us to remain in the body to be used by God to glorify him and to serve one another in love. Life is about God and others. It is not about us. Unless we are focused on who God is and are convinced of his promises we will continue in our pride to worship people, places, and things. And as we worship people, places, and things we will never be satisfied. We will continue to be on a futile search, and in the midst of this futile search we will be most concerned with ourselves, not with God and others.

Getting back to the question at hand, the Bible is clear that death cannot separate those in Christ from the love of God in Christ Jesus. In fact, death is the door to experiencing the love of God in all its fullness. When we enter into glory there will be no more pride and idolatry to take our focus off of the perfect love of God. Be convinced!

How could Paul say in Romans 8:38 that he was convinced that life could not separate us from the love of God in Christ Jesus?

In Hebrews 13:5, God tells those in Christ, "Never will I leave you; never will I forsake you." Life cannot separate us from the love of God in Christ Jesus because God, who is love, has promised that he will never leave us. He is the resurrection and the life (John 11:25). He is the way, the truth, and the life (John 14:6). It would not make sense for God to love us so much that he would give his one and only Son to die for us, and then allow something to separate us from that love. We have already seen that everything that comes our way in life is from the hand of the God who promises to work all things for the good of those who love him and are called according to his purpose (Romans 8:28). Everything that happens in life ultimately happens for the purpose of bringing glory to God. So we are left with the verdict that nothing in life can separate us from the love of God. Life cannot separate us from the love of God in Christ Jesus. Be convinced!

How could Paul say in Romans 8:38 that he was convinced that angels could not separate us from the love of God in Christ Jesus?

Hebrews 1:14 says, "Are not all angels ministering spirits sent to serve those who will inherit salvation?" The angels mentioned here are obviously the elect angels, as distinguished from the demons he speaks of next, who are the nonelect, fallen angels. This verse plainly tells us that God sends his angels, who serve him, to serve us in Christ Jesus. Angels are sent to serve the elect, those who will inherit salvation. Obviously then, angels cannot separate us from the love of

God in Christ Jesus. Rather, they are sent by the perfectly loving God who created them to minister to us. They come in God's love and they minister to us in God's love. Be convinced!

How could Paul say in Romans 8:38 that he was convinced that demons could not separate us from the love of God in Christ Jesus?

> On another day the angels came to present themselves before the Lord, and Satan also came with them to present himself before him. And the Lord said to Satan, "Where have you come from?" Satan answered the Lord, "From roaming through the earth and going back and forth in it." Then the Lord said to Satan, "Have you considered my servant Job? There is no one on earth like him; he is blameless and upright, a man who fears God and shuns evil. And he still maintains his integrity, though you incited me against him to ruin him without any reason." "Skin for skin!" Satan replied. "A man will give all he has for his own life. But stretch out your hand and strike his flesh and bones, and he will surely curse you to your face." The Lord said to Satan, "Very well, then, he is in your hands; but you must spare his life." So Satan went out from the presence of the Lord and afflicted Job with painful sores from the soles of his feet to the top of his head. Then Job took a piece of broken pottery and scraped himself with it as he sat among the ashes. His wife said to him, "Are you still holding on to your integrity? Curse God and die!" He replied, "You are talking like a foolish

woman. Shall we accept good from God, and not trouble?" In all of this, Job did not sin in what he said (Job 2:1-10).

Job obviously was convinced that nothing could separate him from the love of God in Christ Jesus.

God alone is all-powerful. The devil and his fallen angels (demons) can do nothing that God has not foreordained to come to pass. We know this for certain from the story of Job. In Job chapters one and two we see the dialogue between God and Satan. In this dialogue we see that Satan can do only what God has planned for his holy purposes. God sets the boundary lines for everything that happens in life. Nothing can or will happen outside those lines. God never goes out of bounds. Nothing that happens falls outside of God's playing field. Satan is merely a puppet in the hands of Almighty God. History plays out just as God has planned, and God and the elect always win. God even uses Satan's wicked schemes to bring glory to himself. He does this somehow without being the author or approver of sin (Ephesians 1:11; James 1:13; 1 John 1:5).

From the book of Acts we read, "This man was handed over to you by God's set purpose and foreknowledge; and you, with the help of wicked men, put him to death by nailing him to the cross. But God raised him from the dead, freeing him from the agony of death, because it was impossible for death to keep its hold on him" (2:23-24).

Satan's plan devised in evil was ultimately God's plan orchestrated in his holy, just, and loving sovereignty. In Satan's wicked plan of death and destruction, God brought the most glorious good in the history of the world. Satan's plan of death was really God's plan of life.

We also see God's plan worked out in the life of Joseph and his family. God ordained the wicked schemes of Joseph's brothers for good. In Genesis 50:20 we read, "You intended to harm me, but God intended it for good to accomplish what is now being done, the saving of many lives." God ordains everything that happens and has furthermore promised to work all those things for the good of those who love him and have been called according to his purpose (Romans 8:28).

Demons cannot separate us from the love of God in Christ Jesus. If you are in Christ Jesus you are the Lord's, and the devil of hell cannot snatch you out of the Father's hand. As in the case of Job, if the devil inflicts pain into your life, it will come only because of God's holy purposes. God is holy, just, sovereign, and loving; therefore, whatever comes your way finds its ultimate purpose in the hands of a loving, just, holy, and sovereign God. Be convinced!

How could Paul say in Romans 8:38 that he was convinced that the present could not separate us from the love of God in Christ Jesus?

> So, because Jesus was doing these things on the Sabbath, the Jews persecuted him. Jesus said to them, "My Father is always at his work to this very day, and I, too, am working." For this reason the Jews tried all the harder to kill him; not only was he breaking the Sabbath, but he was even calling God his own Father, making himself equal with God (John 5:16-18).

In John 5, Jesus has just healed a man on the Sabbath. God never takes a break from doing good. He does not take a nap, even on the Sabbath. So even in our present, no matter what time of day it is, God is always in control and he is always working all things for the good of those who love him and are called according to his purpose (Romans 8:28).

Whatever is going on in the present is in the hands of the one who was in control of all things before time began. In Genesis 1:1 we read, "In the beginning God..." What a statement! God has always been. God is outside time and space and yet he enters into them. We can look and see that God was in control of all that has happened in the past. Everything that has ever happened has happened for the glory of God. Even the fall of the devil and the human race was ordained for the glory of God, though he is not the author of sin, nor does he tempt anyone to sin (James 1:13-15). We would not know God's love, grace, mercy, holiness, wrath, and justice without the fall. It is God who turns curse into blessing, evil into good, and death into life.

God is unchanging, so the God who was in control of everything in the past is obviously in control of everything in the present. Time cannot separate us from the love of God. No circumstance can separate us from the love of God. Therefore, the present cannot separate us from the love of God. We live in the present and we can trust God in the present because he is always with us. He has promised, "Never will I leave you" and "Never will I forsake you" (Hebrews 13:5). The present cannot separate us from the love of God in Christ Jesus. God was in control of the past, he is in control of the present, and he is in control of the future. Be convinced!

How could Paul say in Romans 8:38 that he was convinced that the future could not separate us from the love of God in Christ Jesus?

"For I know the plans I have for you," declares the LORD, "plans to prosper you and not to harm you, plans to give you hope and a future" (Jeremiah 29:11).

We have already seen that God is good all the time. Whatever plans God has for us for the future, whether they look good or bad to us from our human perspective, we can be assured that they are for the glory of God, and are, therefore good. They are for our good, not for our harm. They are to give us hope, not to lead us to despair.

I can imagine how easy it would have been for Paul to fall into despair when he encountered all the things we saw in 2 Corinthians 11:23-33. The reason Paul did not succumb to despair is that he knew who God was, he knew what God had said, and he knew in the midst of his experiences what was true. He was convinced.

To be prepared for the future we must know who God is now and we must know what he has said. Knowing these two things in the present will enable us to be convinced of the ever-present love of God in the future when we encounter new trials and difficulties (Romans 8:39). May I add that we must not only know who God is and what he has said, but we must truly believe before we can be convinced!

The future cannot separate us from the love of God in Christ Jesus. Be convinced!

How could Paul say in Romans 8:38 that he was convinced that no powers could separate us from the love of God in Christ Jesus?

Jesus said, "I give them eternal life, and they shall never perish; no one can snatch them out of my hand. My Father, who has given them to me, is greater than all; no one can snatch them out of my Father's hand" (John 10:28-29). God is the creator of all. God is greater than all. He is greater than any power. He is all-powerful. If anything or anyone has any power at all, it is only because the all-powerful one has given it to it or him. No power can separate us from the love of God in Christ Jesus. Be convinced!

How could Paul say in Romans 8:39 that he was convinced that neither height nor depth could separate us from the love of God in Christ Jesus?

> Where can I go from your Spirit? Where can I flee from your presence? If I go up to the heavens, you are there; if I make my bed in the depths, you are there (Psalm 139:7-8).

Psalm 139 makes it clear that we cannot escape the presence of God. There is no place, no matter how high or low, where he is not present. God is Spirit. God is love. God is everywhere present. It only stands to reason, then, that nothing can separate us from the love of God in Christ Jesus. Be convinced!

How could Paul say in Romans 8:39 that he was convinced that nothing else in all creation would be able to separate us from the love of God in Christ Jesus?

Look again at John 10:28-29. Jesus said, "I give them eternal life, and they shall never perish; no one can snatch them out of my hand. My Father, who has given them to me, is greater than all, no one can snatch them out of my Father's hand."

Jesus said, "I give them eternal life." The gift has been given. God does not take back the gifts he has given. Jesus said, "They shall never perish." That means they will not and cannot perish. Jesus said, "No one can snatch them out of my Father's hand." That means they are secure in the omnipotent Father's hand. Jesus said, "My Father, who has given them to me, is greater than all, no one can snatch them out of my Father's hand." That means God has given them to Jesus. Do we think God is going to take them from his Son after all that he has done? God is greater than all. Who is going to defeat God? Can anyone snatch us out of the hand of the one who spoke the world into existence?

Because God is the Creator, logically, by definition, he is all-powerful. Once again, any power he has given to anyone or anything is subject to his own. For anyone or anything to have power equal to or greater than God's is ridiculous. If this were the case, there would be more than one God. God cannot re-create himself. If so, the re-created version of God would be created, not the Creator. Everything that exists besides God has been created. Paul plainly tells us that nothing in all creation, which includes everything but God, can separate us from the love of God in Christ Jesus (Romans 8:39). We already know that God, who is love, will never leave us or forsake us (Hebrews 13:5). So this ends the argument. Be convinced!

Let's look again at the awesome promises we have in Romans 8:28-39:

> And we know that in all things God works for the good of those who love him, who have been called according to his purpose. For those God foreknew he also predestined to be conformed to the likeness

of his Son, that he might be the firstborn among many brothers. And those he predestined, he also called; those he called, he also justified; those he justified, he also glorified. What, then, shall we say in response to this? If God is for us, who can be against us? He who did not spare his own Son, but gave him up for us all—how will he not also, along with him, graciously give us all things? Who will bring any charge against those whom God has chosen? It is God who justifies. Who is he that condemns? Christ Jesus, who died—more than that, who was raised to life—is at the right hand of God and is also interceding for us. Who shall separate us from the love of Christ? Shall trouble or hardship or persecution or famine or nakedness or danger or sword? As it is written: "For your sake we face death all day long; we are considered as sheep to be slaughtered." No, in all these things we are more than conquerors through him who loved us. For I am convinced that neither death nor life, neither angels nor demons, neither the present nor the future, nor any powers, neither height nor depth, nor anything else in all creation, will be able to separate us from the love of God that is in Christ Jesus our Lord.

Paul was convinced; are you? I hope and pray that the two-sided coin of pride/idolatry will raise its ugly head less and less and that your life will be marked more and more by humility and worship. When this happens you will increasingly love the Lord your God with all of your heart, soul, mind, and strength, and you will love your neighbor as yourself.

Questions and Prayer

1. Have you been feeling separated from God's love lately? If so, what do you need to do?

2. Are you becoming more convinced of God's love? If so, why? If not, what steps can you take to become so?

3. How would you explain to someone that nothing can separate him from God's love if he is in Christ?

4. Pray that God will make you more convinced of his love. Meditate often on God's character and his promises.

Chapter 9

Love According to God

I hope and pray that you left the last chapter convinced that nothing can separate you from the love of God in Christ Jesus. In this chapter we will look more closely at what love is according to God.

If you were to ask 100 random people on the street to answer the question, "What is love?" I suspect that you would hear quite a few different responses. Likewise, if you were to ask the same people what the Bible means when it says that "God is love," I am sure you would hear a variety of answers.

Scripture tells us that "God is love" (1 John 4:8) and "... the fruit of the Spirit is love..." (Galatians 5:22). In these two verses we see that the Bible plainly teaches us that God is love and that God's kind of love comes from the Spirit of God. God's kind of love is not inherent to human beings. God's kind of love can be present in our lives only as we depend on the Holy Spirit and allow him to produce in and through us what we cannot produce on our own (John 15:5).

What does the Bible mean when it says that God is love? The Bible is not teaching us that love is God. To clarify this, let me give you a few analogies. I can declare to you that my wife is intelligent, but intelligence is not my wife. I am not married to intelligence. One of the descriptions of my wife is that she is intelligent. We say things like this all the time. You may have a dog or cat that you would say is hilarious. But hilarious, unless that is the name of your pet, is not your pet. When the Bible says that God is love it is teaching us that one of the attributes of God's character is love. As a matter of fact, every attribute of God is consistent with the fact that God is love. God is holy, and his holiness is saturated in love. Every attribute of God's character is saturated with love. God does not cease to be love any more than he ceases to be holy or just.

God is always love. He is always holy. He is always just. He always hates sin. He is always in control. He is always all-powerful. He is always all-knowing. He is always everywhere present. God has many other attributes that I have not mentioned, but I wanted to give you a taste of what our great unchanging God is like. I encourage you to study all of God's attributes because God never changes (James 1:17). There is great hope, confidence, and security in knowing that God remains the same all the time. Question #4, "What is God?" from the Westminster Shorter Catechism is answered this way: "God is a Spirit, infinite, eternal, and unchangeable, in his being, wisdom, power, holiness, justice, goodness and truth."[10] God is not like sinful human beings whose character is constantly changing.

If we profess to be in Christ, we obviously should get our definition of love from God and not from the world, the flesh, or the devil. This is elementary, or at least it should be. God is God. We are not. God is love. We are not. God is truth. We are not. Therefore, the truth about what love is or is not must come from God (1 John 4:7-8). God has plainly given us his definition of love in 1 Corinthians 13:4-8:

---

[10] The Orthodox Presbyterian Church, 360.

Love is patient, love is kind. It does not envy, it does not boast, it is not proud. It is not rude, it is not self-seeking, it is not easily angered, it keeps no record of wrongs. Love does not delight in evil but rejoices with the truth. It always protects, always trusts, always hopes, always perseveres. Love never fails.

According to God, we can easily see that love is expressed in action. It is not just a feeling that comes and goes, as many people would say. It is perfect. It is unfailing. It is unending. It is steadfast. It is sacrificial. It is holy. It is based on truth. We are commanded to love God with our entire being and to love our neighbor as ourselves (Matthew 22:37-39).

We cannot love as God defines love in our own strength. We can truly love only in the power of the Holy Spirit as he works in and through us. Scripture tells us to pass on to others the love we have received from God. "We love because he first loved us" (1 John 4:19). Because loving God and others are the two greatest commandments, we need to examine ourselves daily to assess how we are doing fulfilling the aspects of love found in 1 Corinthians 13:4-8.

Are we being patient with those in our sphere of relationships? Are we being patient with God? Are we being patient in the circumstances that come our way in life? *Love is patient.*

Are we being kind to everyone? Are we kind to those who mistreat us? *Love is kind.*

Are we free from the envy of others, for what they have or do not have? *Love does not envy.*

Have we been doing any boasting lately? *Love does not boast.*

How are we doing in the battle against pride? *Love is not proud.*

Do we have a problem with being rude? *Love is not rude.*

Are we selfish? *Love is not self-seeking.*

Do we get easily angered? *Love is not easily angered.*

Do we keep records of wrongs? *Love keeps no record of wrongs.*

Do we delight in evil? *Love does not delight in evil.*

Do we rejoice with the truth? *Love rejoices with the truth.*

Do we protect? *Love protects.* Love bears things for the love of God and others.

Do we trust? *Love trusts.*

Are we full of hope? *Love hopes.*

Do we persevere? *Love perseveres.*

Love never fails.

Anyone of us who has even a little bit of honesty will plainly confess that we struggle with every single aspect of God's definition of love. We will admit that we have failed over and over again.

We have been impatient, unkind, envious, boastful, proud, rude, self-seeking, and easily angered. We have kept records of wrongs. We have delighted in evil. We have not always protected, trusted, or hoped. We have not always persevered. We have failed. Yet God's love never fails nor does it end.

> Hearing that Jesus had silenced the Sadducees, the Pharisees got together. One of them, an expert in the law, tested him with this question: "Teacher, which is the greatest commandment in the Law?" Jesus replied: "'Love the Lord your God with all your heart and with all your soul and with all your mind'. This is the first and greatest commandment. And the second is like it: 'Love your neighbor as yourself.' All the Law and the Prophets hang on these two commandments" (Matthew 22:34-40).

Love is the fulfillment of God's law, which is God's righteous and holy standard. God's standard for us is perfect love toward him and our neighbors in thought, word, and deed for an entire lifetime. We all have broken God's law so many times that we could never keep track of our sin. If you do not believe me, try living up to the definition of love according to God in 1 Corinthians 13 in your thoughts, words, and actions for just a single day. When we see how wretched we are and yet how perfectly loved in Christ we are, we will grow in grace. We have no righteousness to offer God; we have only sin. Jesus has no sin; he has only righteousness.

What an exchange! Jesus takes away our sins and gives us his perfection. We deserve only condemnation because of our sin, but Jesus takes it for us. We do not have the perfection required to enter heaven, but Jesus gives it to us.

Love is based on truth and expresses itself in action; it is not just a feeling. God is love, he has acted in love, and he continues to act in love. His greatest act of love was sending his own Son to die for the sins of the world. Jesus is the greatest gift in the world. God is love and Jesus is God. We know the Holy Spirit is also God and, therefore, he is love. On this basis we can say that God the Father, God the Son, and God the Holy Spirit act in constant, unchanging love. We must get our definition of love from God (who is love), as found in 1 Corinthians 13:4-8.

For those of you in Christ, this is how God loves you, and you can be convinced as Paul was that nothing can separate you from the love of God in Christ Jesus (Romans 8:39). When you are convinced that you are loved like this in Christ you will grow more and more humble. Your idolatry will dwindle. Your worst enemy, that ugly five-letter word, pride, will fade. Your focus and love will become more and more directed toward God and others instead of yourself. When we are consumed with God's love it is hard to be unloving toward others. What a blessing it is to be convinced that nothing can separate you from the love of God in Christ Jesus (Romans 8:39).

> But whatever was to my profit I now consider loss for the sake of Christ. What is more, I consider everything a loss compared to the surpassing greatness of knowing Christ Jesus my Lord, for whose sake I have lost all things. I consider them rubbish, that I may gain Christ and be found in him, not having a righteousness of my own that comes from the law, but that which is through faith in Christ—the righteousness that comes from God and is by faith. I want to know Christ and the power of his resurrection and the fellowship of sharing in his sufferings, becoming like him in his death, and so, somehow to attain to the resurrection from the dead (Philippians 3:7-11).

It is easy to see Paul's humility and his love for Christ. Paul understood God's perfect love. This motivated him to love God and others in the way God commands. He considered everything done in pride and idolatry to be worthless. Paul was being increasingly set free from the ugly, two-sided coin of pride/idolatry, and what a man he became.

Nothing in life compares to knowing Christ Jesus. If we do not treasure Jesus, we are missing out on everything that God created life to be about. We were created to glorify God and enjoy him forever.

> Now all has been heard; here is the conclusion of the matter: Fear God and keep his commandments, for this is the whole duty of man (Ecclesiastes 12:13).

It is very foolish and prideful to reject what the one who created us has said is the only purpose of life.

In the next chapter we will look at how being convinced that nothing can separate us from the love of God in Christ changes everything.

Questions and Prayer

1. How do you define love? Is your definition biblical? Explain to someone else what love is according to God.

2. What aspects of love in 1 Corinthians 13:4-8 do you struggle with the most?

3. Do you understand how pride and idolatry rear their ugly head when we are not convinced of God's love? Think through your own specific struggles concerning this. How do pride and idolatry play out in your own life when you are not convinced of God's love?

4. Do you see why we are humble when we are convinced of God's love? How does humility play out in your own life when you are convinced of God's love?

5. Before you even get out of bed each day, thank God that, because of what Christ has done through his death and resurrection, you are perfectly loved in Christ. Meditate upon God's love throughout the day.

Chapter 10

God's Love Changes Everything

The Beast in the story <u>Beauty and the Beast</u> was very self-focused due to his appearance. This made him fearful, which often led to outbursts of anger. Yet when Belle showed him love through her actions, it changed everything. His ugly pride, which was much uglier than his appearance, was transformed into humility. He was motivated to love after being convinced of Belle's love.

Please do not misunderstand how and when a Christian is to love from my illustration of <u>Beauty and the Beast</u>. We do not have to be loved or feel loved in order to love others. We are commanded to love regardless if others love us in return or not. We are commanded to love our enemies and do good to them (Matthew 5:43-48). We are commanded to overcome evil with good (Romans 12:17-21). Yet, the Bible does teach us that God's love for us does motivate us to love him and others (1 John 4:19). God's love can transform the heart of the most prideful and idolatrous person into a heart of humility and worship.

In the last chapter we saw how constant God's love is. We also looked at his definition of love as summed up for us in 1

Corinthians 13:4-8. If you are in Christ, this is how God loves you. You can be as convinced as Paul was. We have proven from Scripture that if you are in Christ you can and should be convinced that nothing can separate you from the love of God in Christ Jesus (Romans 8:39).

Now let's look at how being convinced that nothing can separate us from this kind of love in Christ can transform our daily lives. We are going to use 1 Corinthians 13:4-8 to help us with this application. If we apply this truth in the power of the Holy Spirit we will see how we can be less full of pride and more filled with humility. We will never be totally free from this struggle with pride this side of heaven. But we can grow in the grace and knowledge of our Lord Jesus Christ. We do not have to be proud people. We can and should be bright, shining lights—people who know we are perfectly loved by God in Christ, and as a result, are humble. We can increasingly live a life of love as we are convinced of God's love for us.

> Love is patient, love is kind. It does not envy, it does not boast, it is not proud. It is not rude, it is not self-seeking, it is not easily angered, it keeps no record of wrongs. Love does not delight in evil but rejoices with the truth. It always protects, always trusts, always hopes, always perseveres. Love never fails (1 Corinthians 13:4-8).

Love is Patient

We know that God is love, so from God's own definition of love, we can say that God is patient. *Because nothing can separate us from God's love, which includes God's patience, how can this love change our lives?*

With regard to our relationship with God, knowing that he is patient with us can give us great confidence that God will never give up on us. He will complete the work he began in our lives (Philippians 1:6). As we saw earlier, God will never condone our sin. He hates our sin. He will discipline us when we need it. Yet he loves us, and nothing can separate us from that love in Christ. We are his forever in Christ. We do not have to fall into discouragement because God will continue to encourage us to grow in grace. We can experience the peace of God because if we are in Christ we are at peace with God. "Therefore, since we have been justified through faith, we have peace with God through our Lord Jesus Christ" (Romans 5:1). It makes no sense to resort to pride (rejecting God's Word) and idolatry (worshipping people, places, and things) when we have a God who is patient with us. When we are convinced that God is patient with us we should be very humble.

When we are convinced that God is patient with us it only makes sense to pass that patience on to others by faith. Part of the fruit of the Holy Spirit is patience (Galatians 5:22). The truth that helps us to be patient with others is that God is patience with us. When I fail to be patient with my wife and children, I need to be reminded of how patient God is with me. Scripture tells us over and over to pass on to others what God has given to us: "Forgive each other just as in Christ God forgave you" (Ephesians 4:32) and "Love one another. As I have loved you, so you must love one another" (John 13:34).

When we are convinced that nothing can separate us from God's love, it only makes sense to be patient in all circumstances. "Give thanks in all circumstances, for this is God's will for you in Christ Jesus" (1 Thessalonians 5:17). When we first look at this verse, if we are honest, we are probably thinking, "Are you kidding, God?" "Yeah, right! You want me to give thanks for *this*? You want me to give thanks for cancer (in and of itself), like cancer is a good thing?" Actually, this verse does not say give thanks *for* what caused the specific circumstances. It says give thanks *in* all circumstances. How can we do this? How can we remain patient? We can remain patient by being convinced that nothing can separate us from the love of God in Christ Jesus (Romans 8:39). We can remain patient because we are convinced that in all things God works for the good of those who love him, who have been called according to his purpose (Romans 8:28). We can be confident that God, who is always good and loving, ordained our circumstances and is using our circumstances to conform us to the likeness of Christ (Romans 8:29). As we trust in the promises we have in Christ, we will be patient and therefore loving.

Love is Kind

Because we know that God is love, from God's own definition of love we can say that God is kind. *Because nothing can separate us from God's love, which includes God's kindness, how can this love change our lives?*

Knowing that God is always kind should lead to humility in our lives. God is always kind and good to his children. Anything that comes our way in life comes from the hand of our truly kind, heavenly Father. He is never mean or harmful. He always does what is best for his glory and for us. Those who have become children of God through faith in Christ should feel very safe and secure in his arms.

Knowing that God is kind to us, we can "be kind and compassionate to one another, forgiving each other, just as in Christ God forgave you" (Ephesians 4:32). Once again the principle applies that what God has given to us must be passed on to others by faith, in the power of the Holy Spirit. Part of the fruit of the Holy Spirit is kindness (Galatians 5:22). As we focus on God's kindness toward us as seen in the gospel, we will be kind, and therefore, loving.

Love Does Not Envy

We know that God is love, so from God's own definition of love, we can say that God does not envy. *Because nothing can separate us from God's love, which includes his never being envious toward us, how can this love change our lives?*

Obviously, God could never envy us. How could he? He is absolute perfection. We, too, can be free of envy when we are resting in the love of Christ. When we are convinced that nothing can separate us from God's love, and when we are convinced that God is always good we will not envy. When we are convinced of these truths, there will be no room for envy. Pride/idolatry says, "God, you do not know what you are doing." Pride/idolatry says, "I should have that position, fame, money, health, looks, gifts, family, etc...." Humility/worship says, "God, you are in control and your will is to be done, not mine." Humility/worship says, "You love me, God, and you have given me the intelligence, appearance, family, talents, and abilities I have for your glory, not mine."

"A man can receive only what is given him from heaven" (John 3:27). What wonderful truth there is in this verse. This statement came from none other than John the Baptist. Talk about a humble man! This man was convinced that nothing could separate him from the love of God in Christ Jesus (Romans 8:39). John said this after being told that Jesus was baptizing many, and after seeing that everyone was leaving him and going to Jesus. John had previously had a huge following and he had baptized many people. Now his ministry was dwindling. Yet he responded not in pride and idolatry but in humility and worship. He knew that God is in control of all things and that "A man can receive only what is given to him from heaven" (John 3:27). What faith! Pastors, please listen up! Do what God commands you to do and leave the results in his hands. Pastors can receive only what is given to them from heaven. Do not fall into idolatry and the fear of man because the church down the road has more members.

This truth applies not only to pastors, but to all Christians. We are called to be faithful in every area of life. We are to do what God commands us to do and leave the results in his hands: "A man can receive only what is given to him from heaven" (John 3:27). As we are resting in God's love, goodness, wisdom, and sovereignty we will not envy others.

Love Does Not Boast

We know that God is love, so from God's own definition of love, we can say that God does not boast. He is not proud. *Because nothing can separate us from God's love, which includes his never boasting or being prideful, how can this love change our lives?*

The root of all sin is pride. God cannot sin. God never practices idolatry. There is a perfect, steadfast, unbroken, unfailing, unending, mutual, loving relationship between the Father, the Son, and the Holy Spirit. Because God is love and does not sin, he never boasts.

Man can and does sin. Man is often proud and idolatrous. We do not have a perfect, steadfast, unbroken, unfailing, unending, mutually loving relationship with anyone. Because man is often proud, he does boast. We do not love when we are prideful. We can be set free from pride/idolatry when we are convinced that nothing can separate us from the love of God in Christ Jesus (Romans 8:39). When we are resting in this truth, we will be humble rather than boastful. Our boasting will be in who God is and what he has done and not in who we are and in what we have done. When we are humble, there is no boasting or pride. May we pray first thing in the morning, "God, thank you that though I sure do not deserve it, nothing can separate me from your love in Christ." Then may we be convinced of this throughout the day. As we are resting in God's love, we will not be boastful or proud.

Love is Not Rude

We know that God is love, so from God's own definition of love we can say that God is not rude. *Because nothing can separate us from God's love, which includes his never being rude, how can this love change our lives?*

God never acts contrary to what is appropriate in every situation. He is always courteous and considerate. He is the standard of perfect behavior. What God thinks, says, and does is always done in absolute perfection. God will never act rudely, inappropriately, or disrespectfully toward us at any time. "The Lord is righteous in all his ways and loving toward all he has made" (Psalm 145:17). We, on the other hand, often think, act, and speak in rude, disrespectful, and inappropriate ways. We often do not consider others when we are focused on our own agenda. We interrupt. We ignore. We do not look at people and truly listen to them. We tempt others by our behavior. We are rude in our use of language and humor. Love does not act in these ways. Love considers the people we are around, the circumstances we are in, and what appropriate thoughts, words, and actions will benefit everyone involved.

This is how God loves. There is never a time when God will be rude to us. There is nothing at all offensive in him. As we are convinced in Christ we will be full of God's love and therefore we will not be rude.

Love is Not Self-Seeking

We know that God is love, so from God's own definition of love, we can say that God is not self-seeking. *Because nothing can separate us from God's love, which includes his never being selfish, how can this love change our lives?*

> Just as the Son of man did not come to be served, but to serve, and to give his life as a ransom for many (Matthew 20:28).

> This is how God showed his love among us: He sent his one and only Son into the world that we might live through him. This is love: not that we loved God, but that he loved us and sent his Son as an atoning sacrifice for our sins. Dear friends, since God so loved us, we also ought to love one another (1 John 4:9-11).

The cross is the standard of sacrificial love. Until we come to the cross by faith we will never know what love is. It is at the cross that we see the horrible offense of our sin. It is at the cross where we see that Jesus died a sacrificial death for those who deserve nothing but eternal hell. The cross is where we find perfect love. The cross proves to us that God is love and that he has no needs. He did not come to get his needs met; he came to meet our need for a Savior.

Because God loves those of us in Christ in this way, how can we not pass this kind of sacrificial love on to others? If we are convinced of God's love, we will be free from being so concerned with others loving and accepting us, which is often idolatrous worship in the form of the fear of man. If we will constantly look at the cross, we will be convinced of God's love for us. We will be convinced that God is for us according to his perfect will. We will be humble and worship and thus not be self-seeking.

Love is Not Easily Angered

We know that God is love, so from God's own definition of love, we can say that God is not easily angered. *Because nothing can separate us from God's love, which includes his never being easily angered, how should that love change our lives?*

> The LORD, the LORD, the compassionate and gracious God, slow to anger, abounding in love and faithfulness, maintaining love to thousands, and forgiving wickedness, rebellion and sin. Yet he does not leave the guilty unpunished (Exodus 34:6-7).

God is never easily angered. He is slow to anger, as Exodus 34 teaches. God does not fear. He does not lose his patience. When God does get angry, his anger is always just and righteous. His anger is never selfish. God does not have a pride/idolatry problem.

Because we struggle with pride/idolatry, we often fear, and as a result of our fear, we lose our patience and we get easily angered. We get easily angered because in our pride/idolatry we think our way is right. We think that the world revolves around us. We are focused on self, and when self does not get its way it becomes angry.

We are to be "quick to listen, slow to speak and slow to become angry; for man's anger does not bring about the righteous life that God desires" (James 1:20). We are not quick to listen in our pride/idolatry. We are not slow to speak and slow to become angry in our pride/idolatry. However, when we are convinced that nothing can separate us from God's love we will not fear and thus not be easily angered.

Love Keeps No Record of Wrongs

We know that God is love, so from God's own definition of love, we can say that God does not keep a record of wrongs. *Because nothing can separate us from God's love, which includes his not keeping a record of wrongs, how can this love change our lives?*

God does not keep a record of wrongs committed by those in Christ in order to accuse them later. "Therefore, there is now no condemnation for those who are in Christ Jesus" (Romans 8:1). If you are in Christ, your sins have been taken away forever. If you are in Christ, God sees you as perfect in his sight. The devil cannot accuse you of anything before God and God will never accuse you. Those in Christ will not have to stand at The Judgment in fear that God will condemn them. "I tell you the truth, whoever hears my word and believes him who sent me *has* eternal life and *will not* be condemned; he *has crossed over* from death to life" (John 5:24, emphasis mine). This verse speaks of eternal life as a present possession for those who believe; it says, *"has* eternal life." It says that those who believe "will *not* be condemned." And it states plainly that those who believe have *already* passed "from death to life." In other words, you were spiritually dead and on your way to hell, but now you have crossed over to spiritual life and are on your way to heaven.

Having this firmly settled in our minds with regard to salvation, I hope now to correct some misunderstandings concerning God's not keeping a record of wrongs.

I have heard some people say that God forgets our sins. They base this on Hebrews 8:12: "For I will forgive their wickedness and will remember their sins no more." If we took this verse in isolation from the rest of Scripture, maybe we would conclude that God forgets our sins. But God is omniscient; he knows everything. God does not erase his memory. What this verse, in connection with the rest of Scripture, is teaching us is that God, in his pure love and grace, will never bring up our wrongs again if we are in Christ because we have already been forgiven. If God's or human beings' minds could be erased of wrongs, there would be nothing great about not keeping a record of wrongs, for no such record would exist. If this were the case, love, in this sense, would be meaningless. There would be no command to obey. God proves that he is love because he never brings up the record of wrongs of those in Christ as it relates to salvation. God does not throw things back in our faces as we do to others and others do to us. He chooses not to bring up our sin again. He has, once and for all, forgiven us in Christ.

God does, however, keep a record of the good and bad that we have done: "For we must all appear before the judgment seat of Christ, that each one may receive what is due him for the things done while in the body, whether good or bad" (2 Corinthians 5:10).

God will and does judge our lives. He does keep a record of the lives of those in Christ for the purpose of rewards and loss of rewards. This judgment has nothing to do with whether we spend eternity in heaven or hell. Let us never forget that

Jesus has already taken the punishment we deserve on the cross. Yet, because God is a just God, he does evaluate everything. The things those in Christ have done with proper motives will be rewarded. If these things were done in the power of the Holy Spirit and for the glory of God, we will be rewarded. Jesus said, "I tell you the truth, anyone who gives you a cup of cold water *in my name* because you belong to Christ will certainly not lose his reward" (Mark 9:41, emphasis mine). The key here is that it be done in *his* name. If these things are done without faith, with improper motives, or for the glory of self, we will not be rewarded.

As judgment relates to those who are not in Christ, God does keep a record of their wrongs for the purpose of bringing them up again at the last judgment (just in case anyone will want to argue with him). "The wages of sin is death" (Romans 6:23a). If God doesn't keep a record of wrongs, how could he judge them? I know this is silly thinking, but people will try anything to deny the truth. God has your record. He knows everything. "This will take place on the day when God will judge men's secrets through Jesus Christ, as my gospel declares" (Romans 2:16). If you have not truly repented and trusted Jesus' death on the cross as payment for your sins, and if you have not believed that God raised him from the dead, God has a list of your wrongs that is beyond counting. It covers not only what you have thought, said, and done that is wrong, but also covers the secrets of your heart and the motives behind all those things you have thought, said, and done.

When the Bible says that love does not keep a record of wrongs, it simply means that love does not choose to bring up others' wrongs against them in a hurtful way. When we are convinced that nothing can separate us from the love of God in Christ Jesus, and when we are convinced that God is for us according to his will, we, too, will not keep a record of others' wrongs.

Love Does Not Delight in Evil But Rejoices With the Truth

We know that God is love, so from God's own definition of love, we can say that God does not delight in evil but rejoices with the truth. *Because nothing can separate us from God's love, which includes his never delighting in evil but rejoicing in the truth, how can this love change our lives?*

The 1 Corinthians 13:4-8 passage, which we are working through, is often referred to and/or held in high regard by both believers and unbelievers alike. Many people, whether saved or not, have this passage displayed upon some decorative item in their home. It is very common, whether someone is in Christ or not, to have these verses read during their wedding ceremony. I do not know of anyone who dislikes this passage. We all want everyone to love us like this, but most of us, if we are honest, are more concerned with others loving us than we are in our loving them. If a person is not in Christ it is impossible to love like this from the heart. The Holy Spirit alone can produce this kind of love, and only those in Christ have the Holy Spirit.

When we look closely at verse 6 of this passage where God defines love with the following words, "love does not delight in evil but rejoices with the truth," many people's love, or at least their understanding of biblical love, grows cold and is really not love at all according to God. As I have stated above, no one outside of Christ can love in the true biblical sense of love. Sure, people outside of Christ can do outwardly good things for other people, have good friendships in general, and have various relationships with family, friends, and others.

Doing outwardly good things and having relationships does not require the power of the Holy Spirit. Biblical love, however, or love that is part of the fruit of the Holy Spirit, can only be produced by the Holy Spirit.

Part of God's definition of love is that it does not delight in evil but rejoices with the truth (1 Corinthians 13:6). Contrary to most people's opinion, God absolutely hates sin. He hates evil. He rejoices with the truth. True love hates sin because sin destroys our lives and our relationship with God and with others. Granted, most people, in their self-righteousness, hate the sins of others, yet they love their own sin and do little about it. If you disagree with me, take the time to read Romans chapters one and two. As a matter of fact, the reason that those who are not in Christ, are not in Christ, is that "they suppress the truth by their wickedness" (Romans 1:18). They do not want to turn from sin to righteousness. If you want to know why your loved ones have not given their lives to Christ, it is because they do not want to repent. They delight in evil and do not rejoice in the truth. It does not matter how nice they are or how outwardly wicked they are. It is the same for all. They do not want to repent. They love their sin more than they love God. They love being wicked. They are miserably content in pride/idolatry. In their pride they want to be their own God, and in their idolatry they love the praise of men more than the praise of God.

Now before those of us in Christ forget where we came from and get puffed up, let us remember that if God had not made us spiritual alive with Christ and given us the gifts of faith and repentance we would still be in the same state as those who are not in Christ. We would still be spiritually dead in our sins, suppressing the truth, and loving our wickedness, if God had not given us spiritual life.

As Christians we need to have a proper view of what God says is love. Love hates all sin no matter how small or big it is. We are never to justify sin in our lives or in the lives of others. We are to stand up humbly for truth. We are to rejoice in the truth regardless of what others think. It is unloving to avoid the truth because we want to be "nice." Likewise, it is unloving to rejoice in the truth if we do not do so with gentleness and respect. Love and truth go together and cannot be separated.

When people are "living in sin" and they call it love, it is obviously not love because sin is opposite of truth; it is evil and unloving. In reality it is lust, which is a form of hate. People who love one another do not use and destroy one another. Any sex outside of marriage (which, by the way, according to God, is reserved only for a man and a woman) is not based on love but on lust, and lust is always self-seeking. Jesus said, "The truth will set you free" (John 8:32). God, because he loves us and wants the best for us, wants us to be free from sin by walking in truth. What we hopelessly seek in sin we find only in truth, which is perfect love and life to the full in Christ. As we are convinced of and resting in God's perfect love in Christ we will not delight in evil but we will rejoice with the truth.

Love Always Protect

We know that God is love, so from God's own definition of love, we can say that God always protects. *Because nothing can separate us from God's love, which includes his always protecting us, how can this love change our lives?*

God has protected those in Christ from eternal conscious torment in hell. This should radically change our lives as we are motivated by God's mercy to obey God out of gratitude for saving us (Romans 12:1). Also, as we learned in the case of Job in chapter eight, nothing can happen to us that God does not permit. God is in control of all things. He has ordained all things for his glory. God protects our name as a child of God because of what Christ has done. We can commit everything and everyone in life to God, for he is all-powerful. We covered this idea of God's protection in detail when we looked at Romans chapter eight. Love protects or bears all things for others. Sin destroys lives, and we can try to protect people by encouraging and admonishing them with the truth. We obviously are to try to protect our children by teaching and modeling the truth. We can help protect the sanctity of life by standing up for all who are helpless and oppressed. We can also help protect by bearing all things with people. We can help carry their burdens and persevere with them. God is the ultimate protector and bearer, but God can use us as a means to accomplish his ends.

"This is how we know what love is: Jesus Christ laid down his life for us. And we ought to lay down our lives for our brothers" (1 John 3:16). As we are convinced in Christ and full of God's love, we will protect or bear all things.

Love Always Trusts and Hopes

We know that God is love, so from God's own definition of love, we can say that God always trusts and hopes. *Because nothing can separate us from God's love, which includes his always trusting and hoping, how can this love change our lives?*

God does not need to live by faith. He does not have to trust anyone. He is all-knowing, all-powerful, and everywhere present. His word is always true. He cannot sin. God does not live by faith or trust as we do because he simply knows and simply is. He does not hope like we do. He knows all things past, present, and future. He ordained the past, present, and future. If God were to live by faith or to trust anyone, he could trust only himself, for he is in control of everything. God does not trust us. "If God places no trust in his holy ones, if even the heavens are not pure in his eyes, how much less man, who is vile and corrupt, who drinks up evil like water!" (Job 15:15-16). We can do nothing apart from him. Jesus said, "I am the vine; you are the branches. If a man remains in me and I in him, he will bear much fruit; apart from me you can do nothing" (John 15:5). We can say that God trusts us only as far as he trusts himself in us. We can do nothing apart from him; yet we can do all things that are within his will through him. "I can do everything through him who gives me strength" (Philippians 4:13).

We are to always trust and believe in God's Word. We are to find hope in God and his word. We are to show our love for God by trusting what he has said. Jesus said, "If you love me, you will obey what I command" (John 14:15). We show our love to others by believing all things. We are to think the best of others. We are to hope the best for them. We are to believe that God can change them and use them. This does not mean that we throw out wisdom. We are not to enable a person, which is not acting in love. We are not to put others in harmful situations by foolishly trusting or believing people we should not. But, in general, we are to give people the benefit of the doubt and think the best of them unless godly wisdom would direct us otherwise. As we are convinced in Christ and full of God's love we will trust that God can use others in powerful ways, and we will believe the best about others and hope the best for them.

Love Always Perseveres

We know that God is love, so from God's own definition of love, we can say that God always perseveres. *Because nothing can separate us from God's love, which includes his always persevering, how can this love change our lives?*

God is the beginning and the end. He is eternal. His very being is one of perseverance. God cannot sin. He never breaks a promise. He completes what he begins. We see God's perseverance in the person of Jesus Christ. Jesus persevered through the trial at Gethsemane. He persevered through the horrible beatings and flogging. He went to the cross and died for our sin. He completed the work the Father had given him, and just before he died he said, "It is finished" (John 19:30). Jesus, in his sacrificial love for his sheep, persevered even unto death. Shall we not persevere for him? To do so we must keep our focus on the one who is invisible. Consider Moses, who, "By faith…left Egypt, not fearing the king's anger; he persevered because he saw him who is invisible" (Hebrews 11:27).

Part of the fruit of the Spirit is faithfulness. As Paul said, "May the Lord direct your hearts into God's love and Christ's perseverance" (2 Thessalonians 3:5). May we persevere in the trials of life as we rest in God's love. May we avoid complaining as we are content in God's perfect love. May we endure trials with patience and thanksgiving for the sake of Christ and those around us. May we be concerned for the glory of God in all situations.

We know that God perseveres with us through our many failings. May we persevere with others through theirs. As we are convinced in Christ and full of God's love, we will persevere in all things.

Love Never Fails

We know that God is love, so from God's own definition of love, we can say that God never fails. *Because nothing can separate us from God's love, which includes his never failing, how can this love change our lives?*

God is all-powerful, all-knowing, and everywhere present. It is impossible for God to fail. His perfect will, will be done. God has ordained all things for his glory. God brings life out of death. If God could fail, he would not be God. In our love for God we do not want to fail. Yet we often do. The amazing thing is that God works even our failings to good (Romans 8:28). Never forget that he has eternally forgiven those in Christ. We are seen as perfect in his sight.

"Love never fails" (1 Corinthians 13:8). We can never fail by loving God and loving others. Regardless of what the world, the devil, and our flesh tell us to do, the right option every time is to love. We can never fail when we love. Even if things do not turn out as we would have liked them to, if we have loved, we have not failed. Love never ends. There will be nothing but love for God and others in heaven. We will no longer struggle with sin in heaven. There will be nothing but perfect love. In the meantime, as we rest in Christ and are convinced of God's love, we will not fail to love.

God's love does change everything. "We love because he first loved us" (1 John 4:19). When we are convinced that nothing can separate us from God's love our lives will be radically changed and we will have victory over the ugly sin of pride, which always leads to idolatry.

Questions and Prayer

1. Write out specific examples of how being more convinced of God's love will change you as you relate to people and to circumstances.

2. In what areas of life are you seeking change? How can being daily convinced of God's love lead to change in these specific areas? Write these specific examples out and meditate on them. Have a preventive plan in place.

3. If you are in Christ but are still struggling with believing that God truly and perfectly loves you in Christ, remember not to trust in your feelings, but in the objective word of God. If you are caught in sin, seek godly counsel and accountability.

4. Pray for specific areas in which you need change in your heart, knowing that being convinced of God's love will produce this change. Trust what God has said and submit to him through obeying his word.

Chapter 11

May You Be Convinced!

I hope you have become increasingly convinced that nothing can separate you from the love of God in Christ Jesus. When you are convinced that God loves you perfectly in Christ, you will, by God's grace, be a bright shining light in the darkness of this extremely prideful and idolatrous world. What a beautiful difference people will see in your life and in your relationships.

Jesus Our Example

May we not take for granted how blessed we are to have the account of the life of Jesus in the Bible. By looking to the Scriptures we can envision ourselves being with Jesus as he walked the Earth. We can see his character shine through the pages of Holy Writ.

His humility shined brightly in how he interacted with people and how he reacted to circumstances. This humility must have been a treat to those who walked with him, as it is to us today as we read the Gospels. Talk about being in the midst of humbleness and contentment! There was not even one nanosecond of his life when he was not controlled by the perfect love of God.

Concerning the humility of Jesus, former Westminster Theological Seminary professor Edmund Clowney wrote, "He was untouched by the defensiveness of insecure pride."[11] There was never any pride or fear of man in the heart of Jesus. He was humble and obeyed God when great crowds surrounded him and he was humble and obeyed God when he was alone. He was never ashamed of God. He never went with the crowd to be accepted. As a matter of fact, on many occasions, he did and said what he knew would bring rejection. At times, even his own family rejected him. On some occasions his own followers disowned him. Most of the Jewish religious leaders and many other Jews and Gentiles did not accept him. He knew when he came into this world that his own would not receive him. Yet he humbly came into the world anyway so that God would receive the glory and those who would believe in him would be saved.

Jesus said, "All that the Father gives me will come to me, and whoever comes to me I will never drive away" (John 6:37). Jesus was rejected while on earth and many reject him today, but he will never drive away nor reject those who come to him.

Expect Persecution

We would all like for everyone to love us. However, the Bible gives us reality. The Bible is real. The Bible does not cover up anything. The Bible is full of truth. The Bible tells us, "In fact, everyone who wants to live a godly life in Christ Jesus will be persecuted" (2 Timothy 3:12). If we are to be all that

---

[11] Edmund P. Clowney, *The Church: Contours of Christian Theology* (Downers Grove, IL: Inter Varsity Press, 1995), 62.

God wants us to be, we are promised that not everyone will love us. Jesus said, "Love your enemies" (Matthew 5:44). This suggests that everyone will have enemies, at least from time to time. We should, of course, never do anything sinful to make enemies; but if we are on the side of truth, those who hate the truth will often choose to be our enemies. Jesus showed nothing but perfect love to all men and yet many hated him. Jesus had enemies even though he was perfect. How can we expect anything different when we are so far from perfect?

Those of us in Christ need to remember where we came from so that we will not fall at this point into pride. Let us remember the words of Paul in Romans 5:10 that tell us, "For if, when we were God's enemies, we were reconciled to him through the death of his Son, how much more, having been reconciled, shall we be saved through his life!" May we never forget that we, too, were once God's enemies and would still be his enemies if he had not chosen to save us by his pure grace.

Maybe you have never thought about it like this, but many people hate the one who created us and gave us life. We all, in at least some sense, hated God before we were in Christ. Jesus said, "If the world hates you, keep in mind that it hated me first" (John 15:18). Jesus, who is God, said the world hates him. Everyone who is not in Christ is of the world. So, on at least some level, everyone outside of Christ hates God. Anyone who is not in Christ is a child of the devil. The devil hates God and so do his children.

Yes, I know many people worship something or someone they call God, and they say they love God. However, the "god" they are speaking of is a "god" they have created, not the God who created them. The God who created us, the God of the Bible, is a loving God, but he is also, at the same time, a holy God who hates sin. The God who created us says that unless we are willing to turn from sin to righteousness and trust Jesus' death on the cross as full payment for our sins and his resurrection as our only hope of eternal life, we will spend eternity in hell. These are the words of the God who created us, and most people hate these words. They hate these words because of their pride. Most people rebel against the true God. They somehow think they can do something to earn or deserve heaven. They hate and despise the true God because they hate and despise his word. God's word has no place in their hearts.

We see this taught plainly in Scripture as Jesus spoke to people who said not only that they believed in God and loved him, but also that God was their Father. These were people who thought they could earn or deserve their way to heaven. Jesus said to them:

> "I know that you are Abraham's descendants. Yet you are trying to kill me, because you have no room for my word. I am telling you what I have seen in the Father's presence, and you do what you have heard from your father." "Abraham is our father," they answered.
> "If you were Abraham's children," said Jesus, "then you would do the things Abraham did. As it is, you are determined to kill me, a man who has told you the truth that I heard from God. Abraham did not do such things. You are doing the things your own father does."
> "We are not illegitimate children," they protested. "The only Father we have is God himself." Jesus said to them, "If God were your Father, you would love me, for I came from God and now am here. I have not come on my own; but he sent me. Why is my language not clear to you? Because you are un-

able to hear what I say. You belong to your father, the devil, and you want to carry out your father's desire. He was a murderer from the beginning, not holding to the truth, for there is no truth in him. When he lies, he speaks his native language, for he is a liar and the father of lies. Yet because I tell the truth, you do not believe me! Can any of you prove me guilty of sin? If I am telling the truth, why don't you believe me? He who belongs to God hears what God says. The reason you do not hear is that you do not belong to God" (John 8:37-47).

In another place we read something similar. Jesus said:

I do not accept praise from men, but I know you. I know that you do not have the love of God in your hearts. I have come in my Father's name, and you do not accept me; but if someone else comes in his own name, you will accept him. How can you believe if you accept praise from one another, yet make no effort to obtain the praise that comes from the only God? (John 5:41-44).

These people wanted to kill Jesus. Why? They wanted to kill him because he told them the truth. He loved them enough to tell them the truth. He knew beforehand that he would be rejected and persecuted. Those of us in Christ should be prepared for people to reject and persecute us, at least to some degree, even if it is only talking negatively about us behind our backs. People are either for Christ or against him. There is no middle ground. You know this is true if you are faithful to living a godly life and to sharing the gospel. People who are outside of Christ are children of the devil, as we have just read, and they despise the true God and his word. If this were not the case, everyone would love hearing the gospel. They would run to you to hear the truth that they are sinners deserving of hell, and they would love to hear you tell them that they must repent and trust Jesus' death on the cross as full payment for their sins and his resurrection as their only hope of eternal life. Yet we know that this is not the case for those outside of Christ. If anyone has ever been offended or just not interested in your loving him enough to share with him that he must be born again to go to heaven and that he cannot earn or deserve heaven, he is a child of the devil and hates, in at least some sense, the true God and his word.

Jesus said, "Blessed are you when people insult you, persecute you and falsely say all kinds of evil against you because of me. Rejoice and be glad, because great is your reward in heaven, for in the same way they persecuted the prophets who were before you" (Matthew 5:11-12). These verses speak of rejection for doing what is right, not to mention all the rejection we experience for doing wrong. If we are honest, we will have to say that we do a lot more wrong than right. Add to this the fact that none of us can possibly love as God commands us to except when we are filled with the Holy Spirit. Once again, if we are honest, we will have to say that we often do not surrender to the Spirit to control our lives. In addition to this, people who are not in Christ can never truly love with proper motives because this love can come only from the Holy Spirit, and those who are not in Christ do not have the Holy Spirit.

Are we starting to see why there is so little true love in this world? Are we starting to see why people desperately try to "find" love in a multitude of ways? Are we starting to see why people do foolish, destructive things to themselves and others in a desperate search to "find" love? Are we starting to see why people worship so many false gods?

God is the Answer

The truth to set all of this straight is that no one but God, the one true God, who is both holy and love at the same time, can love perfectly. Hold on for a moment. Just in case there is any confusion here, I am talking about the God who created us, not a "god" that we have created. The one true and living God exists in three co-eternal and co-equal persons. These three persons are none other than God the Father, God the Son, and God the Holy Spirit. No one can love perfectly at all times except the true God, and that only in Christ.

Saint Augustine, a renowned theologian from the late fourth and early fifth centuries, said, "For thou hast made us for thyself and restless is our heart until it comes to rest in Thee."[12]

Blaise Pascal, a 17th century French mathematician, philosopher, and physicist, said, "There is a God-shaped vacuum in the heart of every man which cannot be filled by any created thing, but only by God, the Creator, made known through Jesus."[13]

Sounds almost like Scripture, does it not? "They exchanged the truth of God for a lie, and worshipped and served created things rather than the Creator—who is forever praised. Amen" (Romans 1:25)

---

[12] St. Augustine, *The Confessions: Book One* (Peabody, MA: Hendrickson Publishers, 2004), 5.
[13] Blaise Pascal, 31 Oct., 2007, ThinkExist.com (31 Dec. 2009), <http://thinkexist.com/comon/print.asp?id=166425&quote=there_is_a_god_shaped_vacuum_in_the_heart_of>.

To what do those who do not have a true saving relationship with God through Jesus Christ turn? The Bible tells us where they turn. In their pride they exchange the truth of God for a lie, and worship and serve created things rather than the Creator. They run from here to there to everywhere. They run from person, to place, to thing, to new idea. Those who do not have a true saving relationship with God through Jesus Christ constantly turn to the creation in idolatrous worship instead of the Creator. They do this because they are spiritually dead.

What about those of us who are already in Christ? When we are not convinced of the gospel and the perfect love we already have in Christ, we, too, foolishly turn to the creation instead of the Creator. When we do this, we commit idolatry and spiritual adultery. Yet God, in his love, gets our attention and brings us back to focusing on who he is and what he has done. And then we think to ourselves, "Why in the world did I exchange the priceless treasure of Christ for fool's gold?" Why did I exchange the truth of God for a lie? Please forgive me, Lord. Thank you that I am a forgiven person in Christ."

When Jesus spoke to the woman at the well in John chapter four, he lovingly showed her the futility of worshipping the creation instead of the Creator. He knew what the woman was worshipping. She was worshipping relationships, or what she thought she could get out of those relationships, rather than the true God. There is no fulfillment in false worship. It always leaves us wanting. Idolatry never holds water. It always leaks (Jeremiah 2:13). True fulfillment is an added benefit or by-product that comes from worshipping the one true God.

A word of caution is necessary at this point. We are never to worship fulfillment or try to "use" God to get fulfillment. That would be a form of idolatry also. However, when we do worship God and trust and obey him we are fulfilled. Jesus, God the Son, is the object of true worship, as is God the Father and God the Holy Spirit. Jesus is the living water. He alone quenches the thirst of the human heart. Those of us in Christ know that living for Jesus is the only way to a fulfilled life. We know this is true based on the objective word of God, and we know it is true in our own personal experience. We have come to experience the life to the full that Jesus promised (John 10:10).

Not only can we be convinced that nothing can separate us from the love of God in Christ Jesus, but we have something in common with all of humanity. We also know what it is to worship the creation in our pride and idolatry instead of the Creator. We know that the creation always leaves us wanting. We know that Jesus is the only way to heaven and the only way to a fulfilled life in the here and now. We can all relate to others as we first listen to them and then share our testimony about how coming to know that nothing can separate us from the love of God in Christ Jesus through the gospel has transformed our lives. However, we must be careful to explain to people that you must come to Jesus for who he is, desiring to live for him, and denying yourself. For many "come" to Jesus only wanting the benefits of God and thus have never truly come to him at all. Here is how Jesus defined eternal life: "Now this is eternal life: that they may know you, the one true God, and Jesus Christ, whom you have sent" (John 17:3). Jesus did not define eternal life as only being saved from hell, experiencing the benefits of God, and seeing your loved ones who are in Christ in heaven. Being saved does include these things, but most importantly, the purpose of our salvation is to humbly worship, both in the here and now and for eternity, the one true God, who deserves all glory and honor.

I pray that the many Biblical passages and verses that appeared throughout this book have helped you become convinced that if you are in Christ you are perfectly loved by God.

When you are convinced of God's perfect love you will fear God instead of man, you will have peace and joy in the trials of life, and you will be free from the foolishness of running after people, places, and things in idolatrous worship. Instead, you will humbly fall at your knees in worship of your Creator, Sustainer, and Redeemer.

May you be convinced of God's perfect love in Christ and may you replace the lies that often creep into your mind with the truth of God. May you worship and serve the Creator who deserves your worship, rather than the creation. And may you teach others by word and example to do likewise.

"Not to us, O Lord, not to us but to your name be the glory, because of your love and faithfulness" (Psalm 115:1).

Questions and Prayer

1. Why was Jesus so humble? In what ways do you think his humility attracted people to him?

2. In what specific ways can you say that becoming more convinced of God's love for you in Christ is changing you? How is this affecting your thoughts, words, and actions? How is this affecting your relationships and how you react to the circumstances of life?

3. How will being convinced that nothing can separate you from God's love specifically free you from your struggles with pride? How will being convinced help you in the midst of rejection and/or persecution?

4. How will being convinced keep you from falling into idolatry or the worship of people, places, and things?

5. How will you share what you have learned about being convinced of God's love? Whom do you know who needs help overcoming pride and the fear of man? Whom do you know who needs to be convinced of God's love?

6. Thank God daily in prayer and praise that nothing can separate you from the love of God in Christ Jesus. Pray that others will be convinced.

References

Clowney, Edmund P. *The Church: Contours of Christian Theology.* Downers Grove: Inter Varsity Press, 1995.

Ferguson, Sinclair B. *The Holy Spirit: Contours of Christian Theology.* Downers Grove: Inter Varsity Press, 1996.

Hoekema, Anthony A. *Created in God's Image.* Grand Rapids: William and Eerdmans Publishing Company, 1986.

Keller, Timothy K. *Ministries of Mercy: The Call of the Jericho Road, 2nd Edition.* Phillipsburg: P & R Publishing, 1997.

Murray, John *Redemption Accomplished and Applied.* Grand Rapids: Wm. B. Eerdmans Publishing Company, 1955.

Pascal, Blaise. 31 Oct., 2007. ThinkExist.com. 31 Dec., 2009. <http://thinkexist.com/common/print.asp?id=166425&quote=there_is_a_god_shaped_vacuum_in_the_heart_of>.

Piper, John. *Let the Nations be Glad.* Grand Rapids: Baker Academic, 2003.

Sproul, R. C., ed. *The Reformation Study Bible: English Standard Version.* Lake Mary: Ligonier Ministries, 2005.

St. Augustine. *The Confessions: Book One.* Peabody: Hendrickson Publishers, 2004.

The Orthodox Presbyterian Church. *The Westminster Confession of Faith and Catechisms as adopted by The Presbyterian Church in America With Proofs Texts.* Lawrenceville: Christian Education and Publications, 2007.

Made in United States
North Haven, CT
24 March 2024